SAMUEL COLERIDGE-Taylor's *Hiawatha*

Oxford KEYNOTES

Series Editor KEVIN BARTIG

Sergei Prokofiev's Alexander Nevsky
KEVIN BARTIG

Arvo Pärt's Tabula Rasa
KEVIN C. KARNES

Aaron Copland's Appalachian Spring
ANNEGRET FAUSER

Rodgers and Hammerstein's Carousel
TIM CARTER

Arlen and Harburg's Over the Rainbow
WALTER FRISCH

Beethoven's Symphony No. 9
ALEXANDER REHDING

Claude Debussy's Clair de Lune
GERMINDER KAUR BHOGAL

Brian Eno's Ambient 1: Music for Airports
JOHN T. LYSAKER

Alfred Schnittke's Concerto Grosso No. 1
PETER J. SCHMELZ

George Bizet's Carmen
NELLY FURMAN

Jean Sibelius's Violin Concerto
TINA K. RAMNARINE

Puccini's La Bohème
ALEXANDRA WILSON

Antonín Dvořák's New World Symphony
DOUGLAS W. SHADLE

Beethoven's String Quartet in C-sharp Minor, Op. 131
NANCY NOVEMBER

Gioachino Rossini's The Barber of Seville
HILARY PORISS

Laurie Anderson's Big Science
S. ALEXANDER REED

Shostakovich's Symphony No. 5
MARINA FROLOVA-WALKER AND JONATHAN WALKER

Samuel Coleridge-Taylor's Hiawatha
BENEDICT TAYLOR

Oxford KEYNOTES

SAMUEL COLERIDGE-Taylor's *Hiawatha*

BENEDICT TAYLOR

Oxford University Press is a department of the University of Oxford.
It furthers the University's objective of excellence in research, scholarship,
and education by publishing worldwide. Oxford is a registered trade mark of
Oxford University Press in the UK and certain other countries.

Published in the United States of America by Oxford University Press
198 Madison Avenue, New York, NY 10016, United States of America.

© Oxford University Press 2025

All rights reserved. No part of this publication may be reproduced,
stored in a retrieval system, transmitted, used for text and
data mining, or used for training artificial intelligence, in any form or
by any means, without the prior permission in writing of
Oxford University Press, or as expressly
permitted by law, by license or under terms agreed with the appropriate reprographics rights
organization. Inquiries concerning reproduction outside the scope of the above should be sent
to the Rights Department, Oxford University Press, at the address above.

You must not circulate this work in any other form
and you must impose this same condition on any acquirer.

Library of Congress Control Number: 2025016033

ISBN 978–0–19–764935–0 (pbk.)
ISBN 978–0–19–764934–3 (hbk.)

DOI: 10.1093/oso/9780197649343.001.0001

Paperback printed by Integrated Books International, United States of America
Hardback printed by Bridgeport National Bindery, Inc., United States of America

The manufacturer's authorized representative in the EU for product safety is
Oxford University Press España S.A., Parque Empresarial San Fernando de Henares,
Avenida de Castilla, 2 – 28830 Madrid (www.oup.es/en or product.safety@oup.com).
OUP España S.A. also acts as importer into Spain of products made by the manufacturer.

Series Editor's
INTRODUCTION

OXFORD KEYNOTES REIMAGINES THE canons of Western music for the twenty-first century. With each of its volumes dedicated to a single composition or album, the series provides an informed, critical, and provocative companion to music as artwork and experience. Books in the series explore how works of music have engaged listeners, performers, artists, and others through history and in the present. They illuminate the roles of musicians and musics in shaping Western cultures and societies, and they seek to spark discussion of ongoing transitions in contemporary musical landscapes. Each approaches its key work in a unique way, tailored to the distinct opportunities that the work presents. Targeted at performers, curious listeners, and advanced undergraduates, volumes in the series are written by expert and engaging voices in their fields and will therefore be of significant interest to scholars and critics as well.

In selecting titles for the series, Oxford Keynotes balances two ways of defining the canons of Western music: as lists of works that critics and scholars deem to

have articulated key moments in the history of the art, and as lists of works that comprise the bulk of what consumers listen to, purchase, and perform today. Often, the two lists intersect, but the overlap is imperfect. While not neglecting the first, Oxford Keynotes gives considerable weight to the second. It confronts the musicological canon with the living repertoire of performance and recording in classical, popular, jazz, and other idioms. And it seeks to expand that living repertoire through the latest music
ological research.

Kevin Bartig
Michigan State University College of Music

CONTENTS

ACKNOWLEDGEMENTS   *ix*

1 Coleridge-Taylor and the Modern Musical Canon   *1*

2 The Path to Fame   *11*

3 Musical Style and Design   *25*

4 Appropriating Others   *53*

5 Identities and Identification   *68*

6 Afterlives   *97*

NOTES   *119*

FURTHER READING AND RESOURCES   *133*

INDEX   *137*

ACKNOWLEDGEMENTS

WHEN I FIRST GOT to know Samuel Coleridge-Taylor's music over two and a half decades ago it was still very much considered (at least in Britain) an outmoded memory of late Victorian and Edwardian culture and its curious musical enthusiasms, something that one should not really admit to being acquainted with, let alone having a sneaking regard for. That a respectable publisher would be interested in publishing a book on *Hiawatha* and its relation to a musical canon (however we might define this problematic concept) would have seemed pretty unlikely back then in the late twentieth century. It is hence deeply gratifying that Coleridge-Taylor's name and music have made a decisive comeback in recent years. The fact that *Hiawatha*, once Coleridge-Taylor's magnum opus, now plays a comparatively smaller part in that rise in reputation than it did in his lifetime is an irony, as I will observe at the end of this book, though it may not be an unfortunate one, since there is so much other wonderful music from this composer that is being rediscovered now.

Anyone working on Coleridge-Taylor owes a substantial debt to earlier researchers, several of whom are independent scholars and historians, who have devoted enormous time and care to correcting the historical record concerning the composer's life and times. In particular, the work of Jeffrey Green over several decades has performed an invaluable service in setting much of Coleridge-Taylor's biographical detail straight. I would like to thank the Keynotes series editor Kevin Bartig and Norm Hirschy at Oxford University Press for their support for the project, as well as the two readers for their extremely helpful feedback on the original proposal and the first draft. James Brooks Kuykendall read a draft manuscript and generously commented upon it, much to the book's benefit; advice was also kindly offered by Berta Joncus, while Damian Taylor helped with two of the images. As always, any errors and oversights remain my own intellectual property.

CHAPTER 1

COLERIDGE-TAYLOR AND THE MODERN MUSICAL CANON

TELL US NOW A TALE OF WONDER . . .

Much excitement was felt as the time drew near to the college concert on November 11. . . By some means, although there was a more or less tacit agreement amongst the students that secrecy was to be observed concerning the work, the excitement leaked out, and music-loving people in touch with the college gained the impression that something unusual would appear at the concert.

So writes Samuel Coleridge-Taylor's early biographer, W. C. Berwick Sayers, in his 1915 account of the first performance of *Hiawatha's Wedding Feast*. On the day of the concert, he relates, the young composer encountered Sir Arthur Sullivan, the elder statesman of British music, in

Samuel Coleridge-Taylor's Hiawatha. Benedict Taylor, Oxford University Press.
© Oxford University Press 2025. DOI: 10.1093/oso/9780197649343.003.0001

the publishers Novello and Co.; Sullivan had got wind of the event and had come to order a score. 'I'm always an ill man now, my boy,' said he, 'but I will come to this concert, even if I have to be carried into the room.'

> When Sullivan arrived in the evening he found the old hall of the Royal College buzzing with a crowded, expectant audience. Every seat was occupied, and people were sitting on the steps of the platform and standing in the passages. . . . When the last strains of the orchestra died away the demonstration of the audience was memorable. Coleridge-Taylor was recalled again and again . . . and next morning he awoke to find himself indeed famous. Every London newspaper devoted considerable space to Hiawatha's Wedding Feast, almost without exception a paeon of appreciation and congratulation, and this was echoed by the newspapers throughout the kingdom.[1]

'Much impressed by the lad's genius. He is a *composer* . . . not a music maker' remarked Sullivan in his diary.[2]

Music histories are accustomed to pinpoint decisive historical events, typically the premiere of a new work, that seem either in retrospect—and sometimes even at the time—to form turning points, effecting major shifts or changes, the emergence of a new voice or changing of the guard. It neatly creates an epic tale, of great works that are also great events, taking part in the unfolding of historical time and reshaping its cultural manifestations. We might think of the 1808 concert at which Vienna and the world first heard Beethoven's Fifth and Sixth Symphonies; the scandalous Paris premiere of Stravinsky's *Rite of Spring* in 1913; or in its own way, Mendelssohn's 1829 revival of Bach's *St Matthew Passion* in Berlin. One such moment in British musical life was surely the 1898 student concert at which the twenty-three-year-old Samuel Coleridge-Taylor, a recent graduate of the Royal College of Music in London, heard his new cantata *Hiawatha's Wedding Feast* presented by the college musicians under the direction of his old composition teacher, Charles Villiers Stanford. 'One of the most remarkable events in modern musical history' is how his former principal at the RCM, Sir Hubert Parry, described it.[3] Despite various shortcomings—the performance itself was a little insecure, and its composer was almost too shy to face the clamouring public at the close—the concert seems to have provided the decisive breakthrough to national, and ultimately international, fame.

Within a few years Coleridge-Taylor had reached an eminence rarely attained before or since by English composers. At a packed Royal Albert Hall two years later, an enthralled audience listened to what, with the addition of *The Death of Minnehaha* (1899) and *Hiawatha's Departure* (1900), had grown into a trilogy of cantatas on Henry Wadsworth Longfellow's popular 1855 epic poem *The Song of Hiawatha*. 'The young composer's triumph was complete' reported *The Musical Times*. 'Rarely, if ever, has such a spontaneous outburst of genuine enthusiasm been witnessed in London at the production of a new work. . . . The pent-up feeling of the deeply moved audience relieved itself in such cheers and shouts of approbation as must have warmed and gladdened the heart of the composer.[4] Indeed, 'We do not think we exaggerate at all in using the phrase "epoch-making" in the English musical Renaissance in connection with "Hiawatha"' wrote the critic for *The Daily Mail*.[5] News of the musical phenomenon quickly spread over the oceans. In the United States, 'Hiawatha mania' took hold, and in 1901 a choral society would be formed in Washington that was named after the composer, whose primary objective was to secure a performance of the trilogy under his direction. Spurred on by their entreaties, Coleridge-Taylor visited the United States three times, his presence proving a talking point not just in musical circles but in national newspapers, and earning him an invitation from President Theodore Roosevelt to visit him at the White House. Coleridge-Taylor would go on to attain worldwide renown—while making his publisher a small fortune along the way—and *Hiawatha* was the composition that propelled him there, and with which he would be associated ever since.

Yet today the event figures rather larger in accounts of Coleridge-Taylor's life than in histories of music—even those confined to that of his nation. Several standard surveys of British music all but ignore the composer, let alone grant him a hallowed place in the unfolding of musical culture.[6] Rival, competing narratives have emerged that overshadow the 1898 *Hiawatha* premiere: of the emergence of the older, but at that time still relatively unknown Edward Elgar just a year later with his 'Enigma' Variations; of Benjamin Britten bursting back onto the post-war British scene with *Peter Grimes* in 1945; even perhaps the curiously new echoes of Ralph Vaughan Williams's *Tallis Fantasia* rising into the vaulted heights of Gloucester Cathedral in 1910. Some commentators have conversely traced the emergence of an 'English Musical Renaissance' back a couple of decades to Hubert Parry, with his (long forgotten) cantata *Prometheus Unbound* of 1880.[7] Arthur Sullivan himself had obtained a comparable success to Coleridge-Taylor in 1862 with the first English performance of his incidental music to *The Tempest*. It is with a curious premonition that we read in his account, 'It is no exaggeration to say that I woke up the next morning and found myself famous.'[8] History is fickle; what future generations choose to remember and single out as significant changes, and Coleridge-Taylor's success is now commonly recorded as noteworthy on merely a personal, rather than national, level. The new dawn that seemed heralded by *Hiawatha* proved short-lived.

A QUESTION OF COLOUR?

What was unusual at the time, and no doubt seems doubly unusual for us looking back, was that all this was the achievement of a young mixed-race composer, whose African heritage—his father was from Sierra Leone—was widely commented upon and, it seems, unmistakable to virtually all who saw him.[9] Recent histories have dissuaded our generation from the erroneous belief that Black migration to Britain was almost entirely a post-war phenomenon, and the significant presence of Black Britons in earlier centuries is now well established. Cases of talented individuals like Ignatius Sancho and George Bridgetower have demonstrated that there were prominent Black musicians working in Britain in the century before Coleridge-Taylor's birth. And yet, that one should obtain such colossal success in the realm of classical music might still seem incredible: a tale of wonder indeed.

To us in the twenty-first century it might seem unlikely, even implausible that a Black composer could have achieved such fame and status. A burgeoning concern to vindicate marginalized figures has usually taken for granted that such marginalization has existed from the start. But Coleridge-Taylor's success in a field commonly associated with elite European culture confounds the usual narrative. How could a former age and culture—one which was at the height of imperial domination over Africa no less—have been so ready to celebrate his accomplishment? But the fact is, it happened. This is no straightforward story of neglect and marginalization, whereby a talented creative artist was excluded from the contemporary music scene owing to their race, gender, or comparable reason, but, quite the contrary, of a palpable historical success. Indeed, if anything, it is our own, more recent era that overlooks Coleridge-Taylor's achievement. In 2003 the British public were asked to vote for the '100 Greatest Black Britons'; the poll was repeated in 2020. Remarkably Coleridge-Taylor was nowhere to be seen on either list.[10] Contrast this with perceptions from his lifetime: in 1904 the *New York Times*, in an opinion piece entitled 'Visit of English Negro Composer Emphasizes American Prejudice', held up Coleridge-Taylor as one of only three people of African extraction who showed the lie to belief in white artistic superiority: the other two named were Alexandre Dumas *père* and *fils*.[11] A year later the prominent African American educator Booker T. Washington would christen Coleridge-Taylor 'the foremost musician of our race', while in 1911 a leading Black newspaper described him similarly as 'the first great Negro composer'.[12] Both white and Black commentators were agreed on Coleridge-Taylor's exceptional status.

Some of this disparity might be accountable to the comparatively insignificant status of classical music nowadays for those 100,000 or so members of the public who voted; it is not Coleridge-Taylor who is marginalized so much as the entire musical culture that he was part of. But still, the contrast across a little over a century is remarkable. And the same goes for what might seem automatic assumptions about the innate racism of the late-Victorian and Edwardian ages. It is not that we should deny there existed a substantial degree of racial prejudice and theorizing in Coleridge-Taylor's lifetime, a great deal of which would be highly unpalatable now. But this was present alongside more liberal viewpoints and progressive politics, and in any case the present age is hardly immune from its own forms of racism either. Douglas Lorimer pertinently warns in this context of the danger of 'colonising the Victorians'—that 'by constructing the Victorians as archetypical "racists", we implicitly celebrate our own freedom from racism.' Consequently, he argues, 'the Victorians have come to stand for the racist Other in binary opposition to our implicit nonracist Self.'[13] The provocation—not to assume we are above reproach now, and the need to explore the nuances of a previous historical age in which race and race-relations were contested no less than now—is surely well taken.

DISPUTING CANONICITY

In this context, *Hiawatha* would appear to be a perfect case study for the purpose of rethinking musical canons in the twenty-first century. The notion of 'canon' called upon here nevertheless requires some qualification. For a start, it is all too easy to speak of 'the canon' as a monolithic, unchanging, and globally uniform entity. Even a cursory examination reveals how blurred the boundary between canonic and non-canonic musics can be, the historical and geographical contingency of many figures who may be canonical at one time or in one place but marginal in another, not to mention sub-canons belonging to specific interest groups within the diverse weave of a larger musical culture. Moreover, as has often been noted, the often overlapping yet distinct concepts of canon and repertory can often be conflated but are conceptually distinct.[14] Some composers of popular classics (like Tchaikovsky or Rachmaninov, for example) may be a central part of the performance repertory but have sometimes proved uncertain inclusions as 'canonical' according to highbrow critics. Equally, there have been plenty of figures honoured more in scholarship than the concert hall. Though most of these points are well-enough established, discussion can sometimes pass over such important nuances and provisos, even making the idea of being canonic weaponized as a term of reproach (as denoting something elite, exclusionary, et cetera), running alongside the no less problematic notion of 'art music' (a heuristic concept whose recent use too readily confuses function with supposed essence). In such a climate, it may indeed be advantageous for music to be seen as non-canonical.

Coleridge-Taylor's music, and *Hiawatha* first and foremost, was indisputably a significant part of a musical repertory in Britain, North America, and the Anglophone world at the start of the twentieth century, and it remained important for specific groups for several decades longer (for middle-class choral societies in Britain, or in historically

Black colleges in the United States, for instance). But was he ever securely or indisputably canonical? A case could probably be made that Coleridge-Taylor was canonical for certain groups in certain periods, if perhaps not widely across a broad and international culture for any long stretch of time. But the fact that his music was a fundamental part of a repertory—i.e. a performing canon—is surely just as important. The success he encountered in his lifetime shows that a Black composer could indeed achieve major prominence within a largely white environment, problematizing what might be an instinctive modern assumption that composers of colour were inevitably excluded from a predominantly white European musical culture. And the subsequent eclipse of his reputation also requires us to examine more critically the varied reasons why this might have happened. Coleridge-Taylor's status may have waned over the twentieth century because of factors other than simply race: the decline in the participatory forms of music making that supported choral works like *Hiawatha*, the reaction against Victorian and Edwardian culture in the wake of both world wars, a snobbery towards more accessible forms of music and the social groups associated with them, et cetera. Even now, reviving Coleridge-Taylor's most famous composition runs into sensitivities that would have barely registered on former ages, especially the problematic constructions of other peoples and races and the appropriation of their cultures manifested in Longfellow's poem— aspects that are in no sense dissolved in Coleridge-Taylor's musical setting.

This choral trilogy forms an ideal musical case study through which we may analyse questions of canonicity, marginalization, identity, and the alternative historical narratives that may arise through expanding the range of composers studied. The reception of Coleridge-Taylor's most famous work offers a fascinating window onto a past age that in many respects remains a foreign and misunderstood period for us. And his modern revival—clearly under way—offers an opportunity to reconsider his life and creative output—music which was for a long time loved by many audiences, and is becoming so once again.

CHAPTER 2

THE PATH TO FAME

HIAWATHAN SKETCHES

In 1897, a work by a gifted young English composer appeared in the concert hall and in print: three character pieces for violin and piano with evocative titles ('A tale', 'A song', 'A dance') and matching epigrams drawn from canto XI of Longfellow's *Song of Hiawatha*—the part named 'Hiawatha's Wedding Feast'. Entitled *Hiawathan Sketches* and published as Op. 16, it seems the first public linking of the names Coleridge-Taylor and *Hiawatha*. The anonymous reviewer in *The Musical Times* (most likely August Jaeger) seems to have had his eye on the composer for a while and was impressed with what he heard:

Samuel Coleridge-Taylor's Hiawatha. Benedict Taylor, Oxford University Press.
© Oxford University Press 2025. DOI: 10.1093/oso/9780197649343.003.0002

Admirers of 'national' music should have flocked to the Salle Erard on the 5th ult. [of last month], when that remarkable young composer, Mr. S. Coleridge Taylor, who, as our readers know, is of partly African descent, gave a concert. The programme consisted of nine new songs, some pieces for violin and pianoforte (*Hiawathan Sketches*) and five Fantasiestücke for string quartet, all of his own composition, interspersed with recitations by the gifted young negro poet, Mr. Paul Dunbar. We cannot find space to do more than generally express our astonishment at a composer barely out of his teens who produces work after work showing remarkable originality in almost every bar. Mr. Taylor, while still a student, reflects neither his teachers' nor anybody else's music, such a case being, perhaps, without precedent in the history of our art. . . . May the fates be kind to Mr. Taylor and give him the fullest opportunities for developing his quite exceptional talent.[1]

Several things can be teased out of this early review, beyond the prophetic connection with the literary work that within a little over a year would make its composer an international sensation. First, Coleridge-Taylor's African ancestry is openly acknowledged, indeed, attention is drawn to it. Significant too is the record of his collaboration with Paul Laurence Dunbar, whom the composer had met just this year; the encounter with the young African American poet would prove critical in catalysing Coleridge-Taylor's commitment to the cause of the African diaspora. At least as prominent, though, is the praise heaped on the composer, in particular the claims for originality and independence from prior models (which are quite remarkable if taken not merely as hyperbole).[2] Hopes were evidently riding high for this young musician.

COLERIDGE-TAYLOR'S EARLY LIFE

Where did this new star in the musical firmament come from? Well, in many ways rather close by. Samuel Coleridge[-]Taylor was born a mile or so away, in Holborn, London, in 1875, and lived his entire life in the London area, mostly around Croydon to the south of the city. Named in echo of the Romantic poet Samuel Taylor Coleridge, 'Coleridge' was the given name he went under to family and friends ('Samuel' was not in fact used), 'Taylor' was his surname, and the two were originally not hyphenated; but early in his career he adopted the hyphenated form by which he is now known, apparently following a printing error.[3] It is with his parents' origins that we have to look a little farther afield. Coleridge was the son of Alice Hare Martin, a white Englishwoman originally from Kent, and Daniel Peter Hughes Taylor a Black doctor from Sierra Leone, who had been studying in England since 1869. Although Sayers's 1915 account claimed Dr Taylor returned to Africa while his son was an infant, his practice having suffered from racial prejudice, more recent research by Jeffrey Green has revealed the story to be a fabrication made to preserve respectably. The parents were never married, and Daniel Taylor was very probably unaware that Alice was pregnant when he sailed back to Freetown over half a year before Coleridge's birth. There is no record of him ever returning, and thus it is almost certain he never met his son.[4] He died in 1904 in the Gambia, comparatively young at fifty-seven but still old enough to have seen his child make a name for himself.[5]

If Sayers constructed a fictional narrative for the sake of middle-class propriety, it appears that Alice and her family were rather less fazed by such matters. Her own mother was unmarried when she was born, and she was raised in the family of Benjamin Holmans, a farrier who was likely her real father, though married to another woman, Sarah Holmans, with whom he already had four children. The young Coleridge was brought up within the Holmans household in Croydon alongside his mother Alice, grandfather Benjamin, and (non-hereditary) grandmother Sarah; his presumed biological grandmother, Emily Martin, remained in contact and used to give gifts to the boy. A decade later, Alice moved in with a railway worker, George Evans, with whom she had three more children—Coleridge's half siblings; again it is unclear whether they actually married.[6]

While the family circumstances appear slightly unconventional on both sides, there seems no doubt that Coleridge was nurtured in a caring and close-knit environment, albeit one of limited financial means (his social background is generally categorized as working class, although his father would certainly have counted as middle class). There is no evidence of his immediate family ever feeling a sense of shame or social stigma about either his birth out of wedlock—maybe unsurprising given their own situation—or indeed the African heritage of his absent father. By his own later account, his grandfather Benjamin was the first to give him a violin and teach him the rudiments of music, and later, probably when Coleridge was around the age of eight, a local musician, Joseph Beckwith, impressed by his abilities, took over the boy's instrumental lessons (Fig. 2.1 shows an early photo of Coleridge with his violin).[7]

FIG. 2.1   A young Coleridge Taylor with violin. *The Musical Times*, 50/793 (1 Mar. 1909), 153.

A year or so later the young musician came to the attention of Herbert Walters, a colonel in the local volunteer battalion, music lover, and philanthropist. According to Walters:

> In the course of conversation one day with Mr. Drage, the headmaster [of the British School, Croydon], he mentioned the fact that he had a little boy of colour in the school, who seemed to be very quick at music. I said I should like to see him, and shortly afterwards arranged to do so. I was much struck with the boy's intelligence and bright, though shy manner. Shortly afterwards, I took him into the choir of St. George's

Presbyterian Church, Croydon, of which I was the honorary choirmaster. From that time I took young Taylor under my special care, and used to have him up to my house in order to teach him some simple theory of music, voice production and solo singing. He was a most delightful pupil, quick, eager and with a wonderful ear. I then practically became his guardian, and looked after him until he came of age. He developed a beautiful voice, and became solo boy of the choir.[8]

As a result of his abilities, Beckwith remembers, Coleridge found himself 'in great demand for At Homes, Soirees, &c', and he was often to be seen playing the violin or singing a solo in the homes, halls, and churches of the Croydon area.[9]

'FAR AND AWAY THE CLEVEREST FELLOW GOING'

In September 1890 at the age of fifteen, through the beneficence of Walters, Coleridge started studying at the Royal College of Music (RCM) in Kensington, where he would remain until the spring of 1897. Initially he was enrolled with violin as his first study, but by 1892 his talents as a composer were becoming evident, and with the support of the principal, Sir George Grove, he switched to concentrate on composition; half a year later he obtained a scholarship. His composition teacher at the RCM was Charles Villiers Stanford (1852–1924), a prominent Anglo-Irish composer and professor of music at Cambridge, who would teach many of the leading figures of the next two generations, including Ralph Vaughan Williams and Gustav Holst. Stanford could be an irascible man—talented, mercurial, but sharp-tongued and capable of riling those around him—though in the case of Coleridge he proved a benevolent teacher and seems to have taken the young musician under his wing, apparently supporting him on occasions when he experienced racial prejudice from other students.[10] To the end of his short life Coleridge showed a respect for his teacher that verged on veneration.

One of Stanford's other pupils at the time was William Hurlstone (1876–1906), who, like Coleridge, commuted to Kensington from the southern suburbs of London, and he and Coleridge became firm friends, often going to concerts together and discussing musical matters. 'I recall that in our student days we each had a musical god' relates Coleridge-Taylor: 'His was Brahms; mine was the lesser known Dvořák.'[11] The impact of Dvořák on Coleridge-Taylor's music from these years is indeed often evident, and the Czech composer would remain an important influence all his life. 'Of composers he would often speak of Dvorak' remembered his friend, Julien Henry in 1912. 'He would say that he should like to write as Dvorak wrote; he considered that Dvorak had exercised much influence on him.'[12] Grieg and Brahms were two others of whom he spoke admiringly, as was in later years Elgar; of contemporary Russian music he appears to have been more critical, though thought highly of some Tchaikovsky.[13]

It had partly been on the strength of choral music that Coleridge was encouraged to switch to composition—he had an anthem published by Novello in 1892 while he was just sixteen—but in the next few years it was primarily with chamber and orchestral music that he developed his voice. The genres involved evoke the gravitation towards German and central European models widespread in the college at the time, though Coleridge's works are distinguished by their melodic attractiveness, harmonic colour, and rhythmic élan, often calling to mind his favoured Dvořák. His official opus 1, a Piano Quintet in G minor (1893) already reveals a fluent command of compositional technique with its harmonic colour, vivacious countermelodies, and highly attractive melodic material integrated within fairly standard formal designs, and these qualities would be developed in subsequent works such as the Nonet, Op. 2 (1893), *Fantasiestücke* for string quartet, Op. 5, and Clarinet Quintet, Op. 10 (both 1895). Some British instrumental music at this time—including pieces by his teachers and contemporaries at the RCM—can come across as worthy but a little dull, lost in a Brahmsian fog, but such criticisms can rarely be levelled at Coleridge-Taylor's works. Stanford himself appreciated the talent he had in his care and promoted it to the celebrated violinist Joseph Joachim—a one-time protégé of Mendelssohn and friend of Brahms and the Schumanns, who had gained the reputation in Germany and Britain as the keeper of the flame for the German classical tradition:

> A mulatto scholar at the College, a boy of 19 with a quite wonderful flow of invention and idea has written a clarinet quintet which I am going to bring to you to see, and if you have time to try. I know you will be pleased with it. . . . His power of melodic invention reminds me a good deal of Dvorak. He is altogether the most remarkable thing in the younger generation that I have seen[.][14]

The quintet was duly played by Joachim and would be published a decade later in Germany by Breitkopf and Härtel.

Already in 1895 a performance had been enthusiastically reviewed in the London musical press, which even at this stage was holding out the young composer, not quite twenty, as a figure to make note of. His Symphony in A minor (designated as Op. 8 but unpublished in his lifetime) would follow in 1896. The first three movements were performed at a college concert in March, but Stanford had been dissatisfied by the finale; it seems that Coleridge accepted his teacher's judgement without question, for he tore up (quite literally) the original movement and laboured without complaint on several further versions in order to satisfy Stanford's criticism.

By the time he left the college in 1897, then, Coleridge-Taylor was already marked out as someone of whom much could be hoped. He had also come to the attention of August Jaeger, an influential editor at the publishing house Novello and Co., who endeavoured to secure contracts for the young composer and promoted Coleridge's music in the press and to other musicians in glowing terms. And it is largely through Jaeger that Coleridge-Taylor gained his first big public success—the premiere on 12 September 1898 of his Ballade in A minor for orchestra at the Three Choirs Festival in Gloucester. Jaeger is best known nowadays as the friend and supporter of Edward Elgar whom the latter would honour in the 'Nimrod' variation of the 'Enigma' Variations, and he had alerted Elgar to Coleridge-Taylor a year earlier as someone who 'will do great things.'[15] At that time Elgar was struggling to obtain a national reputation (indeed Coleridge-Taylor, his junior by eighteen years, had probably more of a name at this stage), but had some sway with the Three Choirs Festival in his native area of west England. Finding himself unable to take on a commission, he recommended Coleridge-Taylor instead to the festival: 'I *wish, wish, wish* you would ask Coleridge Taylor to do it. He still wants recognition, and he is far and away the cleverest fellow going amongst the young men. Please don't let your committee throw away the chance of doing a good act' he wrote to Herbert Brewer, the festival organizer.[16] Jaeger kept up the pressure on Brewer: 'keep your eye on the lad,' he wrote, 'and believe me, he is *the* man of the future in musical England.'[17] Eventually the commission came. Barely two months before the famous *Hiawatha* première in London, Coleridge-Taylor's latest orchestral work 'met with extraordinary success', receiving a standing ovation from the audience and making him the talk of the musical press.[18] The triumph of *Hiawatha* at the Royal College in November was not a bolt from the blue but the consolidation of the success in Gloucester that September.

'A GENIUS I FEEL SURE, IF EVER AN ENGLISH COMPOSER WAS'

What is clear from these early reviews and accounts of the composer is, on the one hand, the enormous promise and pride invested in him as an explicitly 'English' composer and, on the other, the African aspect of his paternal heritage, which was often commented upon, and almost as frequently linked to purported qualities of his music. The last feature might seem significant, as we have seen how Coleridge was brought up entirely in a white environment and given a thorough education in the European classical musical traditions. Until around 1897, there is no evidence he even encountered or closely engaged with African and African-diasporic cultures. But Coleridge-Taylor was mixed-race, and for his contemporaries, steeped in racial theories of the day and drawing on popular conceptions of evolution, his West African biological inheritance ensured that purported 'African' qualities would inevitably be manifested in his music, regardless of whether he had ever been exposed to this culture.[19]

Already we see in the 1897 account of the *Hiawathan Sketches* that the reviewer implicitly links his family background to qualities of the music:

> The violin pieces in slow time seem melodically far-fetched and affectedly vague, though very original; but his quick movements are full of tremendous vigour, strange rhythms, and a wild, untrammelled gaiety suggestive of neither European nor Oriental influence. An altogether new element seems here introduced into our art, the further development of which we shall watch with the keenest interest.[20]

Another common perception was of a distinctive 'barbarism' that could be heard in some of Coleridge-Taylor's music. Early reception of the Ballade exhibits this plainly, speaking of its 'peculiar blending of barbaric and Western modes of expression', 'barbaric gaiety', and 'almost savage character'.[21] For modern listeners the term might well seem a little incongruous applied to the piece; Herbert Antcliffe already remarked in 1922 that 'everybody now admits the incorrectness of these descriptions'.[22] It is hard to believe that racial stereotyping is not primarily responsible for this perception, although there may be more in play than simply an equation of the composer's African paternity with musical 'primitivism', for the reviews also make clear that the music of many Russian and Slavic composers (most prominently Tchaikovsky) were often marked by such 'barbaric' qualities.[23] Here, perceived alterity from an implicit Western European norm (Slavic and African peoples being 'othered' and racially essentialized alike) seems to fuse with a more plausible perception of stylistic affinities—even if the Ballade is arguably influenced as much by French models as by Russian ones.

Equally, however, there is a sense of national pride that Britain had a native-born composer of such quality in its midst, and other reviews at this time insisted just as strongly on the composer's identity as 'English':

> Here we have at last what England has been waiting for ever since she began to repudiate the taunt that she was unmusical, that the creative gift was denied to her musicians. 'Hiawatha' is a creation if ever there was one in our art. It boldly crosses the line that divides the abnormally clever from the simply beautiful, the obviously inspired. . . . this beautiful music of our young countryman.[24]

The two identities—being English and yet remaining in certain respects essentially African—were evidently not seen as incompatible attributes in the same person. This is exemplified in Jaeger's 1897 letter, in which he first praises Coleridge-Taylor as 'a genius I feel sure, if ever an English composer was', before immediately commenting on his racial background, emphasizing his father's Blackness.[25] Indeed, it was the African element that was understood as contributing some of the unexpected flair or 'exotic' appeal that lifted the composer out of being just a run-of-the-mill British musician: 'I suppose you know that his father is a negro. Hence his wonderful *freshness*' Jaeger avers the following year.[26] It is this seemingly intrinsic affinity with what contemporary Europeans considered picturesque, 'primitive' peoples that—in the eyes of his contemporaries—made Coleridge-Taylor particularly suited to treating another topic on such themes: the Native American figure of Hiawatha.[27]

LONGFELLOW'S APPEAL

Why did Coleridge-Taylor turn to *Hiawatha*? From an interview he later gave, 'Longfellow's poem appealed to his fancy as a boy, not by reason of its musical potentialities, but on account of its "funny names." '[28] Its Native American markings—whether real or constructed—might have been as attractive for him as it evidently was for his white colleagues, providing the exotic appeal of a distant people and culture.[29] In choosing this work, moreover, Coleridge-Taylor was tapping into a well-established propensity for setting Longfellow's poetry in Victorian Britain. Despite his low standing in the twentieth century, Longfellow was one of the most respected poets in the Victorian era and 'probably the most frequently set American poet of the 19th century'.[30] The most popular British choral work of the later nineteenth century was Arthur Sullivan's 1886 cantata *The Golden Legend*, based on Longfellow's poem of the same name (Coleridge-Taylor considered it the finest of all British cantatas, and *Hiawatha* would vie with it in public esteem over the following decade), and Elgar had recently completed his *Scenes from the Saga of King Olaf* (1896), following his earlier *The Black Knight* (1889–93), also after Longfellow. The young Frederick Delius had even written a symphonic poem on *Hiawatha* in the late 1880s, though this remained unpublished, unperformed, and almost certainly unknown to Coleridge-Taylor. Most significantly, Antonín Dvořák, a long-time fan of Longfellow's epic, had reportedly been inspired by scenes from *Hiawatha* in composing the inner movements of his Ninth Symphony ('From the New World', 1893), and in the 1890s was considering setting the poem either as a cantata or opera.[31]

Coleridge-Taylor was hardly alone, then, in turning to the American poet. Indeed, he would continue using Longfellow as a source in the years following *Hiawatha*, in works such as the *Blind Girl of Castel-Cuillé*, Op. 43 (1901), and the Five Choral Ballads, Op. 54 (1904–5), whose texts are taken from Longfellow's abolitionist 'Poems on Slavery' (1842). But it is with *Hiawatha* that Coleridge-Taylor's name is inextricably linked. The connection is one that would accompany him over the short span of his professional life, from the *Hiawathan Sketches* of 1897, through the three cantatas and an overture, to the ballet music left incomplete on his death in 1912. The following chapters will look at these in turn, examining both the music and several of the important contexts that intersect with it.

CHAPTER 3

MUSICAL STYLE AND DESIGN

THE BRIGHT TONES OF flute and trumpet outline a simple rising fifth followed by a falling octave. In its rhythmic simplicity and primordial intervallic quality the material evokes a natural, open space, while the orchestral timbre, poised between the martial ring of the trumpet and softer, pastoral shading of the flute, merges the heroic with the bucolic (see Ex. 3.1). There is a freshness and promise to this new musical world. (For Edward Elgar, trying to work on one of his own cantatas at the time, it became an earworm: 'I have Taylor's theme jigging in the vacuities of my head,' he wrote to their mutual friend August Jaeger, who had sent him a copy of the piece several months prior to its first performance. Elgar sent the score back home—but the tune stubbornly remained.)[1] Without pause, the rising fifth

Samuel Coleridge-Taylor's Hiawatha. Benedict Taylor, Oxford University Press.
© Oxford University Press 2025. DOI: 10.1093/oso/9780197649343.003.0003

EX. 3.1   Opening of *Hiawatha's Wedding Feast*

is reiterated, a call to attention, creating an eight-note thematic statement whose rhythmic forthrightness suggests some as yet unrecognized purpose. Under the pedal now formed by its sustained upper note the four horns softly intone a swaying oscillation between dominant and mediant minor; nostalgic, evocative, their introduction of full triadic harmony imparts a new warmth, while the relaxed, non-functional progression opens up regions befitting a tale from some indeterminate past.

   On repetition, the opening idea continues directly into a new rhythmic figure, whose use of a gapped scale and timbral presentation (flutes over simple repeated G major tonic chord in lower wind and violins) suggests a folk-like quality. Syncopation and a switch to the relative minor imparts a mild kick to the concluding stage, which is soon taken up more vigorously in rustic drone fifths in the bass. Their pounding dactylic rhythm (long—short—short) underpins a varied retreatment of the melodic constituents just heard. The chorus rise and with their first entry, 'You shall hear how Pau-Puk Keewis'—the words now revealed as going with that opening rising-fifth theme—we are borne away to become bystanders at Hiawatha's wedding.

So starts the *Wedding Feast*, the first stage in a trio of cantatas that would move from cheerful festivity through tragedy to attain a bittersweet, epic grandeur at its close. A year later, when its successor *The Death of Minnehaha* was premiered at the North Staffordshire festival, Jaeger reported back on how not just the public but many of the seasoned London critics were overcome by the pathos of it all. 'Minnehaha is *beautiful*', he exclaimed. 'It was a sight for Gods to see Bennett & Stratton, & Shedlock & other old stagers "wipe their eye".' (As for his wife, 'she cried half the time'—though Jaeger himself was 'too much concerned about the bad orchestral performance to cry'.)[2] The public were still weeping—and applauding all the more vigorously—the following year, when, with the addition of *Hiawatha's Departure*, the complete trilogy had emerged. 'Who can define inspiration in music?' wrote the *Musical Times* reviewer; 'Who can analyse the qualities in Mr. Coleridge-Taylor's music that touch singers until they can hardly produce their notes, and audiences so that they cannot read their programmes or scores?'[3]

What was it about Coleridge-Taylor's music that made it so captivating, so memorable, so moving, to his contemporaries, to rival composers, battle-hardened critics, performers, and the wider musical public alike? Attempting to explain the musical causes for an emotional effect may be tricky, as the reviewer above acknowledged; but one can at least try to understand something of how the music works. This chapter examines Coleridge-Taylor's music for the trilogy, identifying some of the key components that made it distinctive and were heard to offer a fresh voice on the British musical scene.

FLEXIBILITY OF METRE, RHYTHM, AND WORD SETTING

One of the most basic features singled out for praise was the rhythmic flexibility of the composer's word setting, a quality especially marked given the highly repetitive nature of Longfellow's poetic metre—the ubiquitous 'trochaic tetrameter' (discussed at greater length in chapter 4). 'Although Mr. Coleridge-Taylor has set altogether over 800 lines of Longfellow's poem to music, every one of them, with but the rarest exceptions, consisting of trochaics,' observed one contemporaneous reviewer, 'nothing is more remarkable than the absence of that feeling of monotony which the almost paralysing sameness of the poet's metre might easily have engendered'.[4]

Coleridge-Taylor uses a variety of strategies to obviate the potential four-squareness of Longfellow's eight-syllable lines. The most obvious way of setting four pairs of stressed-unstressed syllables is to set them as even beats in 4/4 time, with metric downbeats corresponding to stressed syllables. This is more or less what Coleridge-Taylor adopts for the opening line | ***You** shall **hear** how* | ***Pau**-Puk **Kee**wis* | (although his written accents create a further emphasis on the first three of every four syllables), Ex. 3.2a:

EX. 3.2A

If it were all like this, the result would soon become tedious, but Coleridge-Taylor continually offers modifications even within a basic 4/4 metre: sprung anapaests (short-long) and syncopations provide a little rhythmic kick; acceleration through a line whereby the second part is set to shorter note values and is therefore completed earlier; ringing the changes with accompanimental stress (such as the orchestra's contrasting accentuation of the weak beats in the opening line above). The metric position can also be altered, the text starting as a one- or two-beat anacrusis (upbeat), especially in cases where the second foot is more verbally significant (*That the* | ***Feast*** *might be more* | ***joyous***), Ex. 3.2b:

EX. 3.2B

Then, the composer can vary the metre: the trochaic feet easily fit as long-short pairs in triple or compound time, with durational emphasis reinforcing the stress (| ***He*** *was dress'd in* | ***shirt*** *of **doe**-skin* |), Ex. 3.2c:

EX. 3.2C

Sometimes the exclamatory quality of a word or line completely takes over (e.g. '*O* | ***Pau**-Puk* | ***Kee**wis*'), with little sense of underlying metre or stress pattern retained (Ex. 3.2d):

EX. 3.2D

All these features are exemplified in the opening sections of the first cantata; they may not seem remarkable in themselves, but given the unchanging poetic metre, the fact that the composer is so successful in avoiding monotony is a considerable achievement.

The choral texture is largely homophonic—the singers singing the same words to the same rhythms at the same time—but includes passages where the separate vocal parts employ different rhythms or are singing different words concurrently. Coleridge-Taylor frequently varies the number of parts in use, contrasting male and female choruses or reducing the texture to a single voice part. There are moments of imitation but no big Handelian fugues or other obvious baroque throwbacks (which had been quite customary in British choral works throughout much of the previous century). Such features, derived from 'learned' European musical techniques and redolent of church music, would have no doubt seemed quite out of place in a work evoking an unspoilt American landscape. It is this balance between accessibility and ease of execution, on the one hand, and textural variety, on the other, that was partly responsible for the music's popularity among choral societies for such a period.

HARMONIC COLOUR

As the account above suggests, the music to *Hiawatha* is replete with numerous colouristic touches that evoke an 'exotic' locale. The harmonic language shows little that is radical for music composed at the turn of the twentieth century, but there is a secure command of chromaticism (voices moving by semitone, progressions to harmonically distant regions, enharmonic switching), seventh chords and other rich, extra-triadic harmonies, and diatonic and modal shifts that marked contemporary harmonic practice.

One of the simplest and most effective ways that Coleridge-Taylor signals the geographical setting is his use of two complementary melodic and harmonic traits: a tendency towards pentatonicism in a major key, and the use of the modal lowered seventh in a minor key. The term 'pentatonic' refers to a five-note, gapped scale, prevalent within many folk traditions across the world. It typically avoids semitones, and within a major-key context it is characterized by an avoidance of the leading note and greater emphasis than customary on the sixth degree of the scale. Indeed, the music can often land on the sixth degree, switching between tonic major and relative minor at ease. One of the opening phrases from the *Wedding Feast* described earlier exemplifies this (see Ex. 3.1, bars 9–10/Ex. 3.4b): though the leading tone is present as a passing note, only five notes are given in all, and the music vacillates between G major and E minor with the pitch E (scale degree 6) especially prominent. A corollary of the latter is a propensity for hearing the two closely related keys as blurred together, which can impart an added-sixth sonority, the sixth degree being added to the tonic major triad. The concluding chorus of the trilogy, 'Farewell, farewell for ever', is a notable example. This added-sixth sonority is characteristic of late Romantic music, often conveying a nostalgic and valedictory quality and associated (as here) with parting. Though not identical, it can be related harmonically to the use of pentatonicism, and demonstrates how Coleridge-Taylor develops a consistent vein of harmonic practice throughout his trilogy.

The other distinguishing trait is the lowered or natural seventh degree in the minor, particularly when forming a descent from the tonic to the fifth, i.e. $\hat{8}-\flat\hat{7}-\hat{5}$. Obvious examples (illustrated here in Ex. 3.3) can be seen in *Hiawatha's Wedding Feast* ('All the bowls were made of basswood', rehearsal 5), *The Death of Minnehaha* ('Forth into the empty forest', rehearsal 19), and the orchestral introduction to the second section of *Hiawatha's Departure* ('From his wand'rings', rehearsal 7), which is later transformed into the refrain 'That you come so far to see us!' (rehearsals 54–57). It imparts a modal touch, again suggesting folk-like origins and/or a certain antiquity. Neither of these features is unique to *Hiawatha* or indeed to its composer. And Coleridge-Taylor's primary source for them was likely only indirectly American music, at best. Both of these features were important elements of Antonín Dvořák's musical language but were especially pronounced in his music composed in and closely associated with America—works such as the Symphony No. 9 ('From the New World') Op. 95, String Quartet Op. 96, and String Quintet Op. 97, all dating from 1893 during the composer's two-year sojourn in the United States. Pentatonic elements are evident in the opening themes and scherzos of both chamber works and in the second theme and slow movement of the symphony; the lowered seventh is manifested in the symphony's introduction and transition theme and in the central episode of its

EX. 3.3   Minor-key melodic ideas with natural lowered seventh (marked with *) in *Hiawatha*

slow movement, as also in the slow movement of the quartet and trio of the quintet.

Dvořák, as we know, was Coleridge-Taylor's musical hero, and the latter would certainly have known the 'New World' Symphony as it was performed several times in London in the 1890s (including an 1896 performance at the Royal College). But it is also very likely that he would have known some of Dvořák's published statements on Native American music (the composer's interviews with New York newspapers were quickly relayed to the British musical press, and Coleridge-Taylor was an avid reader of music journals during his student years, as his wife relates).[5] In these, Dvořák is reported as claiming that while writing his symphony he was influenced by Native American ('Indian') music: 'I have not actually used any of the melodies', he divulges: 'I have simply written original themes embodying the peculiarities of the Indian music, and, using these themes as subjects, have developed them with all the resources of modern rhythms, counterpoint, and orchestral colour.[6] In making the further—no doubt debatable—claim that he found Native American 'practically identical' to African American music, and moreover that 'the music of the two races bore a remarkable similarity to the music of Scotland', he also links this more identifiably with specific musical qualities. Pentatonicism is generally assumed to be the trait he is thinking of, which is also found in some of the African American spirituals that Dvořák heard and is widespread in Scottish music (think of 'Auld Lang Syne' or the Skye boat song). It furthermore suggests why the lowered seventh (a characteristic of many spirituals) might become linked with Native American practice, if the musics of the two groups were conceived as collapsing into each other. It was also well known at the time that part of the 'New World' Symphony was inspired by certain (unnamed) scenes from Longfellow's *Song of Hiawatha*.[7] In incorporating these harmonic and melodic traits into his *Hiawatha* music, then, Coleridge-Taylor was taking up elements that served as musical signifiers for Native America. Irrespective of whether they actually had a close connection with indigenous musical practice, non–Native American audiences would have still understood these elements as connotative of it.

More generally, the harmonic style of *Hiawatha* is marked by an ease of modulation and local transfer between tonal centres. An instructive example is given by the orchestral introduction to the third part, *Hiawatha's Departure*, which provides a concise compendium of Coleridge-Taylor's typical harmonic facility. The opening sounds appear to brush away the sorrow of the preceding cantata, with a bracing B major chord in the wind instruments injecting a breath of fresh air ('spring had come in all its splendour' the soprano will soon inform us). The trilling F#-G# in the upper voices turns in the third bar into a familiar I–vi–I oscillation, but its repetition immediately falls to the minor mode (B minor), which itself oscillates with its own flattened submediant, G major. This in turn switches abruptly to its relative, D major, and in the passage that follows, B minor and D major vie for the upper hand. Such is the modal equivocation that it is only with the entry of the solo voice in bar 31 that D major is confirmed as the real goal of the introduction. Even now, though, modal instability continues throughout the ensuing scene. The reprise of the song's opening music in D major (rehearsal 4 bar 5— henceforth labelled 4:5) is inflected with the B♭ borrowed from the parallel minor, with the result that the tonic is constantly coloured by the minor mode, preparing for the D minor at its end describing the still grieving Hiawatha. There is a continual game of reinterpretation operating in this opening section: the initial B major quickly decays to B minor, and this in turn becomes understandable as an off-tonic opening to the real tonic of D major. Yet as the entire cantata will end in B major, it is arguable that the initial B major was the true global tonic after all. (The overture that Coleridge-Taylor wrote for the trilogy, discussed in chapter 5, plays with this same duplicity.)

What we hear in this opening section is how easily and adeptly the composer switches between parallel and relative modes and their associated harmonies: B major and G# minor, B minor and G major, D major and D minor all change into one another with utmost fluidity. The effect is redolent of the still uncertain emotions accompanying the progression from the cruel winter of the preceding cantata to the beauties of spring described by the first song, in which only the sorrowing Hiawatha, 'speechless in his infinite sorrow', stands apart. There is little here that is intensely chromatic, let alone dissonant; rather, the idiom relies on continual transformations of familiar consonant triads to closely related keys, but in such a way that the course of the music is never too predictable and maintains a suppleness and fluidity.

Two other prominent aspects of Coleridge-Taylor's language are worth briefly highlighting here. First is the incorporation of modal elements and progressions to common diatonic harmonies; this category might also include a propensity for plagal closes and the final tonic being approached or secured through means other than traditional dominant-tonic motion, such as by a prolonged pedal or from the submediant. (This chapter's final section will discuss this feature in greater detail.) The other, quite distinct trait, is the composer's propensity for semitonal modulation over successive passages at a medium-scale level. Numerous sections of the three cantatas exhibit an underlying motion by chromatic step. The most famous part of the entire trilogy, the tenor solo 'Onaway! Awake, beloved!' that sits at the centre of *Hiawatha's Wedding Feast*, is a case in point: approached from F major, the key in which the preceding music had concluded (one flat), the first verse of the song itself is in G♭ major (six flats), but this creeps up to the tonally distant G major (one sharp) for the second verse, before returning to G♭ in the final abbreviated reprise. The semitonal shifts between F, G♭, and G continue in the ensuing music for some time. It appears to be one of Coleridge-Taylor's personal ticks or fingerprints: the slight shift imparts a new tonal colour and showcases the composer's technical sleight of hand while keeping the music in practically the same register for the singers involved. In some instances a rising tonal sequence might be conceived as creating a steady rise in tension (a familiar device in nineteenth-century opera, termed a 'rosalia'). An example of this is found early in the same cantata in the description of Pau-Puk Keewis leading up his dance, starting in F major ('He was dress'd', rehearsal 25), rising to G♭ ('On his head', rehearsal 27) and thence to G ('Barr'd with streaks', rehearsal 28:7), before reverting to F♯ minor to describe the mystic dances that were performed ('First he danced', rehearsal 31).

Musical commentators often seem to assume that the most radical and theoretically noteworthy techniques are responsible for creating the music's aesthetic or expressive highpoints. But some of the most affecting parts of *Hiawatha* are not those that show the composer pushing the boundaries of harmonic usage at all but, quite the opposite, arise from a restraint of means, where an unexpected simplicity of utterance is all the more moving. This is surely the case for the central cantata, *The Death of Minnehaha*, which as we saw was the one that expressly reduced contemporary audiences and performers to tears. Here the framing of the narrative within the material of the bleak E minor orchestral introduction, which returns just before the final section (rehearsal 62), creates an overriding mood of tragedy, in which the story recounted within is already heard as hopeless. But while customary features such as the minor mode, slipping chromaticism, and harsh dissonances (like the diminished sevenths and minor ninths for the dying Minnehaha's despairing cries of 'Hiawatha!' after her absent husband, rehearsals 38–42) are expressively used for conveying the famine and the suffering it causes, perhaps even more affecting is the use of the major mode in the sections following Minnehaha's death, where the minor might have been a more obvious recourse for a composer. In passages like the wailing 'Wahonomin! Wahonomin!' (rehearsal 43) and the music leading up to the soprano's 'Then he sat down still and speechless' (rehearsal 50) the unexpected major colouring and melodic simplicity creates a bittersweet quality, a tenderness that is all the more touching for being too late. When the fateful chromatic slipping of the framing E minor music returns near the end of *Hiawatha's Departure*, transformed into the major mode, the affect is similarly one of transfiguration. Pathos can be created through simple means, and Coleridge-Taylor certainly knew how to achieve this.

MANIPULATION OF MOTIVES AND THEMATIC CONSTRUCTION

One of the most distinctive aspects of Coleridge-Taylor's music to *Hiawatha* is how economically and resourcefully he reworks the thematic material. The earlier parts of the trilogy in particular are marked by the constant reuse and transformation of a small number of motives heard near the start. This attribute was recognized and remarked upon by contemporary critics. Reviewing the vocal score prior to the first performance, *The Musical Times* observed:

> 'Hiawatha's Wedding-Feast,' which occupies fifty-eight pages of octavo vocal score, may almost be said to be constructed upon a few simple tunes, which are rhythmically the direct musical expression of the words. But such is the art of our young composer . . . that, in spite of the almost unlimited repetition of such phrases as—

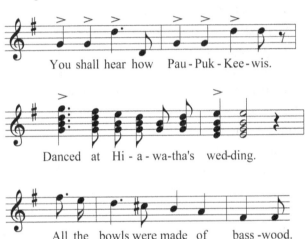

> —no feeling of monotony is allowed to mar our enjoyment [of] the music. These and other phrases are so spontaneous, and they are subjected to so many clever metamorphoses, that the ear never grows tired of them.[8]

It is possibly exaggeration to claim that *all* the music for the first cantata is derived from its opening ideas (as an enthusiastic reporter in the *Washington Post* asserted of the first 12 bars), but there is undeniably great motivic consistency over the *Wedding Feast* and most of the themes can be related more or less closely to these initial ideas.[9] As the trilogy continues, the thematic resources on offer become less frugal: a single cantata of about thirty minutes' duration can stand such economy, whereas trying to extend this material to generate three quite contrasting pieces that play for two hours would likely overtax it. Nevertheless, the two sequel cantatas employ several overt references to earlier music as quotation or transformation, creating a sense of narrative progression or arc over the three works.

Coleridge-Taylor's deployment of such thematic economy in *Hiawatha's Wedding Feast* in part reflects his conservatory training: the derivation of a wealth of material out of only a few small ideas upholds an ideal of organic interconnection, which by the turn of the century had become associated with exacting standards of musical sophistication and considered a hallmark of 'symphonic' composition. (The *Musical Times* critic observed how in this respect the composer had 'taken a valuable lesson from his master, Professor Stanford'.)[10] But there is also a sense in which such repetition and variation neatly complements the subject matter. A mosaic-like reuse and continual variation of small melodic fragments is associated with folk music practices, and, equally, with artistic stylizations of folk music (it is seen particularly clearly in the nineteenth- and early twentieth-century Russian repertory, from Glinka and Balakirev to Rimsky-Korsakov and Stravinsky). Longfellow's text itself employs numerous repetitions and duplications, meant to invoke oral storytelling practices. In some cases, Coleridge-Taylor simply repeats or reclothes ideas;[11] in others he more intricately rearranges thematic constituents or suggests family affinities between different yet related themes. Either way, the result is both a display of technical proficiency (showcasing his credentials as a serious composer of classical music) and a stylized formal analogue for the 'native' subject matter.

An exemplar can be given by the opening sections of *Hiawatha's Wedding Feast*. The brief orchestral introduction sets out at least three short ideas (Ex. 3.4): (*a*) the opening fifth motive (bb. 1–3), which will be recalled and transformed in both succeeding cantatas; (*b*) the quasi-pentatonic scalar pendant (bb. 9–10); and (*c*) the vigorous dance at rehearsal 1 which seems to take elements of the two preceding motives in its initial decorated fifth,

EX. 3.4   *Hiawatha's Wedding Feast*, opening motives

followed by quicker conjunct descent (the hint of pentatonicism here will be brought out later) and characteristic closing syncopation.

These three thematic ideas will be immediately taken up in the ensuing chorus, the first two clothed with the words of lines 1–3, the third as a type of linking refrain. This chorus itself exhibits ternary (ABA) organization on multiple levels: initially in contrasting a central G minor variant between two G major statements, and then on a higher level by using this whole passage as the opening section of a larger ABA design. A central section is implied by the change of key to B minor and an apparently new idea (motive *b2*, 'All the bowls were made of basswood', rehearsal 5), but in fact this material has been subtly prefigured some bars earlier in a continuation to the opening section's internal reprise

EX. 3.5   *Hiawatha's Wedding Feast*, derivation of motive *b2* from *b*

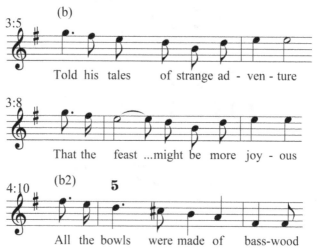

at rehearsal 3 ('That the feast might be more joyous'), which was derived quite clearly from the opening motive *b* (see Ex. 3.5). Following the larger reprise at rehearsal 7:15, this material returns as a type of dissolving coda over a long tonic pedal, rounding off the opening chorus.

While the following sections introduce more distinctively contrasting material, there are often common elements shared with the opening cluster of motives (the theme at rehearsal 13 sounds new, for instance, though it can conceivably be derived from the preceding $b2$ material; it will itself attain greater prominence as an important idea in the ensuing cantata *The Death of Minnehaha*, heard in the introduction and thereon throughout). More significant, however, is surely the fact that the opening material is never absent for long. The pattern that emerges is of fresh material constantly being balanced by the recall of earlier ideas, often transformed into new yet recognizable guises, creating a mosaic effect of continual reuse and recombination. Thus, $b2$ is heard again at rehearsal 16:8 to round off the connecting passage; *a* is reworked at rehearsal 18; a variant of *b* given at rehearsal 19; *a* and *b* provide the basis for the music between rehearsals 21 and 24; and *c* returns at rehearsal 24. Pursuing such motivic accounting further would be easy but tedious: the point is that the texture is filled with the recurrence of these characteristic melodic ideas. It would be quicker to point to the significant themes that are not transparent versions of the opening ideas: the swinging 6/8 theme at rehearsal 25 ('He was dress'd'), the soft, hymnlike passage at rehearsal 41:3 ('Then said they to Chibiabos'), the tenor solo 'Onaway! Awake, beloved!' (rehearsal 45). And even these can be shown to be derived from preceding themes (the first to *b*; the second to the opening of *c*), or incorporate motivic reminders within the texture (motive *a* within 'Onaway!', rehearsal 47:3).

The following two cantatas are musically more extensive (the concluding *Hiawatha's Departure* is indeed significantly longer), and while they rework several thematic ideas over their course, they are less tied to the same few motives. In *The Death of Minnehaha*, for instance, the orchestral introduction provides material for several subsequent passages. As the opening chorus ('Oh, the long and dreary Winter!', again ternary in design) leads directly out of the introduction and employs the same material, the two passages should probably be understood as part of the same larger opening section. A major-key variant of its main theme is heard twice subsequently, however, to describe with bittersweet effect the dying Minnehaha ('And the lovely Minnehaha', rehearsal 16; 'In the wigwam with Nokomis', rehearsal 32), while a subsidiary phrase of the introduction (bb. 10–18)—the chromatic slipping figure first heard in *Hiawatha's Wedding Feast* (rehearsal 13)—returns at rehearsal 42. The main theme recurs in its original minor-key form in 'Thro' the far resounding forest' (rehearsal 25:4) and during the funeral scene ('And at night a fire was lighted', rehearsal 58:2), finally being recalled prior to the last section (rehearsal 62) as a framing device. The melody that will be heard here in this closing passage, ' "Farewell", said he, "Minnehaha" ' (rehearsal 63) was itself prefigured at rehearsal 31, and conceivably forms a major-key transformation of the opening theme. Another important theme, used in several places, is that first presented at 'Forth into the empty forest' (rehearsal 19, shown earlier in

Ex. 3.3), being heard again as Hiawatha vainly scours the forest for sustenance (rehearsal 27), and then transformed into an ostinato that underpins the powerful funeral scene ('Then they buried Minnehaha', rehearsal 55). The prominent fifths and forthright rhythmic construction suggest a possible affinity with the trilogy's opening theme (*a*) without literally recalling it. Several of the themes in *Hiawatha's Departure* likewise appear related: many of them feature a prominent neighbour-note motive ($\hat{5}$–$\hat{6}$–$\hat{5}$) and corresponding emphasis on degree 6, which could conceivably be traced back to the opening bars.[12] There are also a few examples of larger thematic recall within the piece, while as discussed below, the final sections in turn bring back several themes from the previous cantatas.

LARGER CONSTRUCTIVE PRINCIPLES AND DRAMATURGY

This brief account suggests a significant recourse to their opening ideas throughout the latter two cantatas, but there is nonetheless a substantial amount of contrasting material in both and the effect is less single-minded than the *Wedding Feast*. Moreover, in the first cantata the thematic material employed is often of a more 'exotic' flavour, giving an impression that we are onlookers or auditors of a picturesque native scene being depicted; in the later cantatas there is a greater sense that the human, expressive elements of the story have taken over and the characters are arguably less marked as foreign or 'other'. The main theme of *Minnehaha*, for instance, is akin to a slow sarabande, with its two-beat emphasis on the second bar of each 3/4 phrase conveying a solemnity and dignified pathos; there is little that is conceivably exotic to this, in contrast to the colourful opening of *Hiawatha's Wedding Feast.*

This shift in emphasis is also reflected in the dramaturgy of each cantata and how this develops over the broader span of the three. The first, the *Wedding Feast*, is essentially a choir-based work: it presents an epic narration, albeit in the collective voice of the chorus. The one exception is the tenor solo, 'Onaway! Awake, beloved', a detachable aria that stands somewhat outside the rest of the music, and even this is a stylized performance ('diegetic' music in theoretical jargon), as the crowd is begging Chibiabos to sing at this point. There is little sense of personal identification with the characters but rather the imagined witnessing of a colourful pageant that is recounted (and part re-enacted) by the chorus. The second, *The Death of Minnehaha*, introduces further solo voices, a baritone and soprano, both of whom assume more dramatic roles, though the chorus is still the principal protagonist and serves as the primary narrative voice. Both soloists are introduced early on as the allegorical figures of Famine ('Buckadawin') and Fever ('Ahkosewin'), but thereafter the baritone relates the speech of Hiawatha (rehearsals 22, 63), while the soprano takes on the characters of Minnehaha (rehearsal 35) and Nokomis (rehearsal 43), besides subsequently acting as a narrator (rehearsal 50). Both singers recount not only the characters' direct speech but also the narrative framing of this (for example, 'And the foremost said, "Behold me!"', or '"Hark!", she said, "I hear a rushing"'), personifying the character whilst ultimately serving as narrator for them. Although the cantata as a result is more ostensibly dramatic, and there are obvious implied visual elements such as the quasi-cinematic switching between concurrent events—Minnehaha dying in the wigwam, while far away in the frozen forest Hiawatha desperately searches for food—the overriding narrative mode keeps it within the bounds of an unstaged cantata rather than suggesting a need for theatrical presentation. In the final work, *Hiawatha's Departure*, solo voices and their linked personas become more prominent still and push the cantata ever closer to becoming a virtual stage work. All three soloists are given significant roles: the soprano is least individualized, performing the opening song celebrating the arrival of spring and serving as narrator a little while later (rehearsal 36), but the tenor takes on the roles of Iagoo and the Black-Robe chief, and the baritone is reserved for the part of Hiawatha. There is a much greater proportion of solo music, and the emphasis on the chorus as principal carrier of the narrative is correspondingly reduced.

In other words, across the three cantatas there is a degree of movement away from the chorus and epic narration towards closer identification with individual protagonists and dramatic presentation. The baritone, in particular, becomes more or less identified with the figure of Hiawatha by the end. The result is, admittedly, no more operatic than Mendelssohn's 1846 oratorio *Elijah*, one of the cornerstones of the British choral tradition in the nineteenth century; it is nevertheless understandable how staged performances of the trilogy with scenery were possible in following decades (see chapter 6).[13]

In larger design, too, the three cantatas strike a balance between sectional construction and continuity that is not untypical of British choral works in this period. Individual

MUSICAL STYLE AND DESIGN

sections are usually more or less distinct, using a given group of performers (chorus, soloist/s, or mixture of the two) and based on the same musical material. There are occasional 'numbers' (most obviously 'Onaway! Awake', which was often detached as a stand-alone aria) and a few set pieces or extended scenes (the funeral scene towards the end of *Minnehaha*, several parts of *Hiawatha's Departure*). As we saw in the account above of *Hiawatha's Wedding Feast*, initial sections are commonly arranged as ternary structures, and themes can proliferate and return in later sections, creating a larger continuity and cohesion. While cadences are often found at the end of a section, there is seldom a sense of a complete break, though a few rhetorical non sequiturs are employed (thematic recall can override a slight hiatus, for instance, as at rehearsal 28 in *Hiawatha's Departure*). Orchestral passages provide prefatory and linking functions in all three.[14] At the larger level of the individual work there is a sense of recall in the final part of each cantata, though this can be achieved through varied means, being primarily tonal in the first, tonal and thematic in the second, and tonal and cyclically thematic in the final work (described in more detail at the end of this section).

Probably the most ambitious attempt to interpret the trilogy formally was made by August Jaeger in the analytical notes written for a 1903 Royal Choral Society performance in the Royal Albert Hall. In these, Jaeger claims that the three cantatas as a whole can be conceived as a four-movement symphony, the *Wedding Feast* constituting the first movement, *Death of Minnehaha* forming a slow movement, and the longer *Hiawatha's Departure* splitting into a scherzo and finale.[15] The final cantata does admittedly consist of two distinct parts, owing primarily to the fact that Coleridge-Taylor draws on two cantos from his source text, namely, the second half of XXI and all of XXII—unlike the previous two cantatas, which each set a single canto, namely, XI ('Hiawatha's Wedding Feast') and XX ('The Famine'). While the two passages selected are adjacent and run on in narrative from each other (the former, 'White Man's Foot', foretells the arrival of the white settlers through Iagoo's eyewitness report and Hiawatha's vision, the latter presents their coming), there is clearly a temporal break of a few months over the final two cantos. In canto XX, the long and bitter winter gives way to spring, and we join the text with 'Came the spring with all its splendor';[16] at the start of canto XII it is described as a 'pleasant Summer morning'. The musical division that Jaeger perceives, however, does not occur over the break in Longfellow's text (rehearsal 28 in Coleridge-Taylor's setting) but some little while prior to it, at rehearsal 19, as Hiawatha prepares to tell his vision. The symphony was a prestigious form at the time Jaeger was writing, and the analogy was no doubt intended to flatter the composer; but it may be best to disregard this reading, since it does not appear to elucidate much either musically or in terms of narrative structure.[17]

One final point to consider here is the question of intra-opus thematic recurrence. With a few small exceptions, thematic recall between the three cantatas is manifested in two principal forms: (1) the use of the work's opening idea as a type of leitmotiv, and (2) the extended references to music from the first two cantatas in the final part of *Hiawatha's Departure*. The recurrence in the second

MUSICAL STYLE AND DESIGN

and third cantatas of the opening 'fifths' motive (*a*) from *Hiawatha's Wedding Feast* appears a salient event, clearly highlighted to the listener and hence potentially signalling some wider meaning. It recurs in *The Death of Minnehaha* at rehearsal 22 for Hiawatha's appeal to 'Gitche Manito the Mighty' to 'Give your children food, O Father!' But it is significantly more prevalent in *Hiawatha's Departure*. It is first heard at rehearsal 19 following Iagoo's account of the 'people of the white faces' and just before Hiawatha tells his disbelieving people 'True is all Iagoo tells'; again as the Native Americans are awaiting the arrival of the approaching white-faced strangers (rehearsals 30 and 33), and then following Hiawatha's exhortation to protect the guests, 'For the Master of Life has sent them / From the land of light and morning!' (rehearsal 73, repeated at 74). Finally, the motive is thundered out in the brass in the very last bars as a culmination of the whole cantata cycle, the music having come full circle. On casual hearing it could seem to be employed simply as a loose unifying device, but in light of its textual associations it does seem to become linked with Gitche Manito ('the Great Spirit, the Master of Life') and/ or destiny—namely, the arrival of European settlers, presented here as inevitable and the wish of the native gods.

The recall of music from the earlier cantatas near the end of *Hiawatha's Departure*, meanwhile, serves both formally and narratively to round off the cycle as a whole and imbues the closing minutes with a pronounced valedictory quality. The final scene effectively starts at rehearsal 67 following the description of the day's lengthening shadows, whose soporific stupor creates an anticipation of something significant about to occur. The chorus at this point, 'From his place rose Hiawatha', recapitulates the hymnic theme from the *Wedding Feast*, first given at rehearsal 41 ('Then they said to Chibiabos') and recalled at rehearsal 70 ('Tell us now a tale of wonder'); in fact the recall has been anticipated in the passage immediately preceding, which brings back that theme's continuation ('Sing to us, O Chibiabos', rehearsal 42). On the previous two occasions this music was heard, the chorus were requesting to be entertained by a song and by a story, and its recall now not only brings us back to that happier earlier time, on Hiawatha and Minnehaha's wedding night, but it might almost insinuate by association the insubstantiality of everything we have been listening to, as if the intervening course of events is itself—or will soon be—nothing more than a tale. Tonally, too, the passage slips from its opening E major through E minor to G major, linking back to the principal keys of the preceding two cantatas. Hiawatha's ensuing solo, 'I am going on a distant journey' (rehearsal 71) in which he bids farewell to his people, remains in the *Wedding Feast*'s tonic of G major and reworks characteristics of its motives *a* and *c*; the opening motive (*a*) recurs directly in the following passage (rehearsals 73–74), being heard again just before the final chorus (rehearsal 83), and given one last time in the closing bars.

Following this, introductory material from *The Death of Minnehaha* re-emerges (rehearsal 82), the same motive that had briefly prefaced that cantata's own final section (rehearsals 62–63), though now in a major-key transfiguration of that earlier bittersweet farewell. The added-sixth harmony opening the closing chorus ('Farewell, farewell for ever!', rehearsal 83) forms the last and most nostalgic of this final cantata's thematic metamorphoses of its opening $\hat{5}$–$\hat{6}$ oscillation. And the final approach to the tonic is likewise attained plagally, avoiding any perfect cadential close. The chorus's ultimate B major harmony is reached via a colourful deflection to the flattened submediant (♭VI; rehearsal 87:5). This harmonic progression has already a history in the trilogy, recalling the same notable ♭VI swerve in Hiawatha's apostrophe 'To the Islands of the Blessed' in the conclusion to *The Death of Minnehaha* (rehearsal 66; his assertion that 'my task will be completed' is proleptic of the actions of the final cantata). But while the flattened submediant at the end of *Minnehaha* is a C major chord, in the B major context of *Hiawatha's Departure* this same shift to ♭VI alights on G major harmony, thereby touching for one final time on the tonic of *Hiawatha's Wedding Feast*, the opening key of the trilogy. And the very last progression heard in the orchestra—a plagal minor-subdominant to tonic—enfolds the remaining E minor of *Minnehaha* into the B major sunset of *Hiawatha's Departure*.

CHAPTER 4

APPROPRIATING OTHERS

HIAWATHA'S DEPARTURE

Near the end of Longfellow's epic, in the final canto of his eponymous *Song*, Hiawatha sees a vision of the possible future. He sees his people—not just the Ojibwe but Native Americans as a whole—scattered and divided,

> *Weakened, warring with each other;*
> *. . . the remnants of our people*
> *Sweeping westward, wild and woful,*
> *Like the cloud-rack of a tempest,*
> *Like the withered leaves of Autumn!*

This 'darker, drearier vision' is a warning of things to come, of what might be. What has prompted Hiawatha's clairvoyance is the arrival of the Pale Faced strangers—white

Samuel Coleridge-Taylor's Hiawatha. Benedict Taylor, Oxford University Press.
© Oxford University Press 2025. DOI: 10.1093/oso/9780197649343.003.0004

settlers, sending their envoys in front. Hiawatha has also foreseen this coming, and its consequences. He had beheld 'all the secrets of the future'

> ... *the westward marches*
> *Of the unknown, crowded nations.*
> *All the land was full of people,*
> *Restless, struggling, toiling, striving,*
> *Speaking many tongues, yet feeling*
> *But one heart-beat in their bosoms.*

But as he sees it, it is not the white men who are in any sense responsible for the destruction of native America. Quite the contrary: the downfall of his people is what will happen if Native Americans are 'forgetful of my councils', which at this point consists of welcoming the strangers with open arms 'as our friends and brothers'. And in his farewell speech, Hiawatha exhorts his people to receive and take care of the new arrivals:

> *Listen to their words of wisdom,*
> *Listen to the truth they tell you,*
> *For the Master of Life has sent them*
> *From the land of light and morning!*

The Master of Life, 'Gitchie Manito', seems to espouse something like manifest destiny. That these justifications and exonerations of settler expansion are put into the mouth of a Native American figure by a white poet may appear more than a little problematic for our age. Still, Coleridge-Taylor set this entire text, uncut, in the third and final part of his *Scenes from The Song of Hiawatha, Hiawatha's Departure.*

The result, for anyone following the words at this point, may make for uncomfortable listening.[1]

WHENCE THESE STORIES?

It is easy nowadays to overlook Henry Wadsworth Longfellow (1807–82) as a poet and forget the enormous status he held in his lifetime, both in his native United States and in Victorian Britain. 'Longfellow doesn't "count" as a "good" poet' observes Brad Fruhauff ruefully: 'he represents a kind of domesticated, nonintellectual, conservative school of poetry that was basically "too naïve" to outlive the nineteenth century', whose sentimentality and associations with middlebrow Victorian culture were completely out of sympathy with twentieth-century literary canons (like, to an only milder extent, Coleridge-Taylor's most famous work based on his poetry).[2] If Coleridge-Taylor's reputation fell off markedly over the twentieth century, Longfellow's went off a cliff edge. Yet in his day he was considered the preeminent American poet of the century, and his popularity in Britain was such that he was commemorated in Poets' Corner in Westminster Abbey (a space generally reserved for British authors). Longfellow was 'not merely the most popular American poet who ever lived but enjoyed a type of fame almost impossible to imagine by contemporary standards,' claims poet and literary critic Dana Gioia. He 'exercised a broad cultural influence that today seems more typical of movies or popular music than anything we might imagine possible for poetry'.[3]

Nowhere is this more evident than in the success of *The Song of Hiawatha*, his most celebrated work. Published in 1855—the same year as Walt Whitman's first *Leaves of Grass*—*Hiawatha* sold 5,000 copies in its first five weeks, 10,000 over the next six months, and within four years sales had reached nearly 50,000.[4] For a period, Hiawatha-mania gripped white America, and the poet himself would grow weary of the number of recitations that were put on in the following years. The cultural influence of the work would have remarkable reach and longevity, and would play an important part in constructing a vision of the Native American as 'noble savage' for decades to come.[5]

Hiawatha is ostensibly based on Native American sources, though Longfellow's work is the confluence of a bewildering number of literary influences: classical antiquity, Scandinavian Eddas, British and German Romanticism, and the Finnish *Kalevala*. Most of the 'Indian' material was derived from the work of Henry Rowe Schoolcraft (1793–1864), a white geographer, Indian Agent for the US government, and early collector of Native American stories. As Alan Trachtenberg explains:

> the poem is in no sense an actual translation. There is no original 'song of Hiawatha'; what we have is Longfellow's fabrication out of legends already wrought into literary English by Schoolcraft and others. With indispensable help from his half-Ojibwa wife, Schoolcraft at Sault Ste. Marie learned enough Algonquian to copy down oral performance as written text, and in the process bowdlerized and altogether converted native storytelling into finished and respectable English narrative. Bemused by Schoolcraft's indiscriminate and near-chaotic ensembles of tales and beliefs, Longfellow nevertheless drew freely from his writings.[6]

The name Hiawatha itself was taken from an Iroquois of that name, a real historical figure, though Longfellow applied it to the protagonist of the stories Schoolcraft had arranged around a semi-mythical Ojibwe warrior called Manabozho, and created an idealized, white-settler vision of the virtuous native who brought peace and prosperity to his people—bequeathing the gifts of agriculture, medicine, and writing—and would finally welcome the European settlers and the new religion of Christianity that they brought.

Perhaps the most famous—or infamous—feature of Longfellow's creation is the poetic metre he employs, what is known as 'trochaic tetrameter' or lines of eight alternating stressed and unstressed syllables (four trochaic 'feet'). The best-known lines of the poem, appearing in canto III and repeated at the opening of the final canto, later set by Coleridge-Taylor in *Hiawatha's Departure*, provide a convenient example:

> **By** the **shores** of **Git**che **Gum**ee,
> **By** the **shin**ing **Big**-Sea-**Wat**er

The strongly marked rhythm and repetitive verbal formulations (as shown in this example, Longfellow especially likes providing both native words and the English equivalent for an object) are quite idiosyncratic: for some readers it imparted a hypnotic, incantatory quality, though others would soon tire of the repetitive nature and simple (**dum**-dum **dum**-dum **dum**-dum **dum**-dum!) rhythm. Numerous parodies were made, even within weeks of the original publication, and Longfellow's verse would become pilloried as doggerel in the twentieth century.[7] (It is this innate repetitiveness in the source text that critics recognized when they praised Coleridge-Taylor for his varied text setting and skilful avoidance of rhythmic monotony.)

Trochaic tetrameter is unusual in English verse (which tends more towards unstressed-stressed syllable pairings or 'iambs'). It was thought by Schoolcraft to be 'not ill adapted to the Indian mode of enunciation', and although this would now be considered an inadequate representation of Algonquian-Ojibwe language, the metre certainly imparts a sense of 'otherness' that could well have been conceived by a Euroamerican audience as exotic and plausibly 'Indian'. But trochaic tetrameter is also famous for its association with the Finnish national epic, *The Kalevala*, compiled by Elias Lönnrot in the second quarter of the nineteenth century, and this proves to have been Longfellow's main source in writing *Hiawatha*. The original Finnish text is not strictly speaking in trochaic tetrameter—common to both are simply the lines of eight syllables, the first of which is accented—but one of its early and most influential translations, Anton Schiefner's of 1852, adopted the more regular trochaic metre in German, and the association has stuck. Longfellow, a talented linguist and translator from numerous European languages, had obtained some exposure to Finnish while visiting Sweden in 1835, the year that Lönnrot published the first version of the *Kalevala*. But the principal source was nevertheless Schiefner's German translation of the work, which he read shortly before embarking upon *Hiawatha*. The link was noted by critics at the time, and Longfellow was quite open about the influence: 'In "Hiawatha" I have tried to do for our old Indian legends what the unknown Finnish poets had done for theirs, and in doing this I have employed the same meter, but of course have not adopted any of their legends'.[8] (Though much longer, the *Kalevala* exhibits a similar organizing principle, unifying a wide range of folk stories and oral variants around a handful of protagonists, and breaking off, like *Hiawatha*, with the arrival of Christianity in the country.) Hence the 'Indian Legend' that Longfellow presents is mediated through a wide range of literary influences, many of them European in origin.

APPROPRIATING CULTURE, WHITEWASHING HISTORY

At the start of *The Song of Hiawatha*, Longfellow takes some care to make a number of claims: that the following poem is taken both from the natural landscape and from the native people that inhabit it (the two seem to be symbiotically linked), and as a result it is natural, unspoilt, uncorrupted, free from artifice, childlike in its tones. Indeed, these qualities implicitly guarantee its authenticity.

> *Ye who love a Nation's legends,*
> *Love the ballads of a people,*
> *That like voices from afar off*
> *Call to us to pause and listen,*
> *Speak in tones so plain and childlike,*
> *Scarcely can the ear distinguish*
> *Whether they are sung or spoken; –*
> *Listen to this Indian Legend,*
> *To this Song of Hiawatha*

As we saw, though, for all its appropriation of Native American material, *Hiawatha* is nothing if not highly constructed. Longfellow himself knew well enough that his hero 'lived purely in the realm of fancy'.[9] The claims he makes are a familiar literary manoeuvre. What are they doing here? What is the cultural work or function that his poem seeks to accomplish and that its consequent popularity reveals it successfully carried out?

As Brad Fruhauff argues, *Hiawatha* attained its enormous success in part because it fulfilled a cultural need, namely, 'to provide the requisite mythic foundations for the young country.'[10] A traditional literary form for creating such a myth was the epic, as Virgil had done for Rome, James Macpherson attempted for Scotland with his semi-fabricated Ossian stories, and Lönnrot had recently achieved for Finland. Longfellow's task was thus to invent an epic history for a new people in an old land: the United States had its founding story—a mythology in a way—in the events of the Revolution, but this was too recent, too genuinely historical, to form a true epic. So, without a significant history, the settlers had instead to take poetic possession of the American landscape, of its geography, a natural space standing as surrogate for primordial time. Hence, rather than an epic, if anything Longfellow's work tends towards another genre—the pastoral, with its prizing of the natural landscape and the 'works and days' of those who live alongside and within it. 'The pastoral aspect performs much of the poem's cultural work, which is in fact the work people had wanted an epic to do, namely, grant them a sense of belonging and connection to an ancient land.'[11]

The problem, of course, was that there already existed a people in this land, an indigenous population that had its own myths and culture. Longfellow's obvious solution was to appropriate the stories of those already there in the land. His poem performs 'a kind of efficacious trick whereby the poet "re-connects" readers to a past that was never theirs.'[12] But the result was a further dilemma: such annexation of a culture looks especially dubious if that culture is still there to show the illegitimacy and inauthenticity of the appropriation. So the indigenous population needed to have all but vanished, to have made way of their own accord for the new settlers. In literature this vanishing act can be made to sound both inevitable and more or less a fait accompli, while at the same time imparting a gentle nostalgia to the events, relegating them to the past while they are in fact still a problem of the present—what Patrick Brantlinger has aptly termed 'proleptic elegy'.[13] Tellingly, as early as 1824, Longfellow had asserted that it was not a matter of *if* but '*when* our native Indians, who are fast perishing from the earth, shall have left forever the borders of our wide lakes and rivers'—in other words, gone and consigned to history, leaving behind a 'classic ground' imbued with their memory, a fertile space for poetic reflection on the part of the white settlers.[14] As Fruhauff sums up,

> In *Hiawatha* Longfellow employs the myth of Native American immediacy to nature (their pastoral priority), as well as their disappearing image, in order to poetically institute an American literariness premised on an intimate connection with the history and language of the land they were in many ways still settling. The demands of legitimizing a colonial people's rights to displace the prior inhabitants of a land while those inhabitants remained among them provided Longfellow with an impetus for rewriting Native American

persons as disappearing ('Westward! westward!') in the wake of Hiawatha.[15]

Thus *Hiawatha*

> uniquely made available to a people, in their own idiom, a sense of connection with a land and a community that was disappearing, even as we understand it to be a poem fraught with the pathos of a nascent nation seeking to understand itself, and with the tragedy of its founding at another nation's expense.[16]

In appropriating Native American stories, then, Longfellow is laying claim to a prehistory for the settlers. Moreover, in implying that Native American society was already in a state of decline before the Europeans started settling the country, and putting words into their mouths expressly welcoming the new arrivals, Longfellow is letting the indigenous population appear to legitimate the takeover— passing the baton on to the new inhabitants, who inherit not just the land, but the stories and culture that seemingly belong so inextricably to it.[17] The strategy may seem ethically dubious; but it was highly effective.

FAREWELL, O HIAWATHA!

One of the most iconic visual manifestations of the craze for *Hiawatha* was a work by the German-born, US-naturalized painter Albert Bierstadt. 'The Departure of Hiawatha' (Fig. 4.1) depicts the hero leaving his people at the end of canto XXII, sailing away in his birch canoe, whispering 'Westward! Westward!' as he merges into the light of the setting sun reflected on the waters of Lake Superior.

FIG. 4.1   Albert Bierstadt, 'The Departure of Hiawatha' (c. 1868), oil on paper, $6^7/_8 \times 8^1/_8$

Bierstadt gave the painting to Longfellow at a dinner he held in his honour in London in 1868; it is now housed at the Longfellow-Washington House in Cambridge, Massachusetts. This evocative picture, oil on paper, is in fact fairly modest in scale (at around 6 x 8 inches it is nothing like the enormous canvases of the Rocky Mountains Bierstadt is most famous for); if there is sublimity implied by the scene, it is kept in check by the domestic scale. Almost as noteworthy is how the image is framed: four pieces of wood, crossing at each corner, impart a natural, rough-hewn, almost 'primitive' quality (a stylized fantasy of native craftmanship perhaps), mildly belied by the varnished veneer. The vision of a vanishing native America is packaged in an appropriate form, a nostalgic piece of settler confectionary. The (non-Native American) viewer is invited to marvel at the splendour of the landscape, feel a gentle pang of nostalgia at the ancient people vanishing before their eyes, and perhaps, as spectator of the image, take the place of the onlooking Native Americans.

So Hiawatha sails off into the sunset, to the Isles of the Blessed and the Land of the Hereafter. He will not live to see the dreary vision of his people scattered and deposed turn into a reality, driven ever 'westward!' by the encroaching pale-faced strangers. But Longfellow and Bierstadt did live to see it, as did Coleridge-Taylor. And for modern audiences, more aware of the unpalatable consequences of American colonialization and greater sensitivities on behalf of the displaced peoples, this may give pause for reflection when encountering the final cantata. By 1900, no one could deny the utter devastation of Native American society, one that had been depicted so fancifully, so opportunistically in *The Song of Hiawatha*.

We do not know what the composer himself thought (if anything) about the wider political ramifications of the text. 'The essential beauty of the poem', he is reported to have claimed, 'is its naïve simplicity, its unaffected expression, its unforced idealism', and we recall what first attracted him to the text was the 'funny names'.[18] Nothing here suggests a significant concern with the political implications that would so concern us now—a position that is altogether unsurprising given Longfellow's reception at this time in Britain. Some commentators have argued that as someone from a minority group and having been subject to racial discrimination himself, Coleridge-Taylor may have identified with the Native Americans. For Michael

Pisani, 'perhaps his magnum opus, exotic trappings notwithstanding, was intended to be understood as a beachhead in the battle for mutual tolerance between peoples of diverse cultural and racial origins'.[19] As we will see in chapter 5, the sufferings of the Native Americans could be and sometimes was read as an allegory for the plight of those from the African diaspora. There is no obvious reason why Coleridge-Taylor, along with many of his white compatriots, might not have shared a widespread sympathy for the situation of the Native Americans while still appreciating the story primarily for its colourful locale. The extent to which compassion for the indigenous population translated into significant criticism of the settlers is nevertheless unclear from the documentary sources we have.

The musical setting does not tell us much about any putative political persuasions on the part of its composer either. Even granting the relative semantic indeterminacy of music, and the consequent possibility for projecting quite a wide range of verbal meanings onto it,[20] it is hard to read any obvious anticolonial critique in the music given to Hiawatha's vision of the 'westward marches' of the settlers, or manifest irony in Coleridge-Taylor's setting of the black-robed missionary's evangelizing speech (though the text at this point could conceivably lend itself to such an interpretation, as will be discussed below). In fact, settlers and natives alike appear to be treated sympathetically. Coleridge-Taylor's music for the vision episode blends a heroic quality—which comes to the fore fitfully amidst much instability in the description of the modern United States in the making—with an overriding mood of melancholy tinged with tragedy reflecting the implications for the native population. At 'Then a darker, drearier vision' the music turns from sharp keys to D minor—the key of the great funeral scene from *The Death of Minnehaha*—and the rising octave figure in the melodic line might well recall the material used earlier there, only now in place of the natural modal seventh there is a more anguished, chromatic descent to follow.[21] Rather than emptiness and grief there is ominous foreboding, and this passage brings the first part of the cantata to an unexpectedly sombre close. The principle of associative tonality might further connect Hiawatha's vision of the onward path of the pioneers to the missionary's reference to Jesus ('her blessed Son, the Saviour'), both of which feature a brief confirmation of the unusual, 'bright' key of C# major within a larger section that decays to D minor.

Nevertheless, some more recent writers have claimed a conscious ironic intent in parts of the final cantata. Meirion Hughes and Robert Stradling, in their provocative 1993 account of the English Musical Renaissance, assert that '*The Song of Hiawatha* insinuated an anti-colonial and (mildly) anti-white message . . . Coleridge-Taylor's work stimulated the sympathy of the middle classes for dangerous causes.' Tellingly, no evidence is offered to support the reading either in terms of musical treatment or the composer's stated views; it seems to be based simply on the authors' understanding of Longfellow's poem, in which, they claim, 'Longfellow stresses the heroic endurance of a free people, arguing that colonisation and cultural extinction are synonymous. . . . The European invaders are greeted with stoic acceptance. Preaching of the Christian message . . . is presented in an ironic vein.'[22] To say that this is an idiosyncratic reading is putting it mildly. Nothing in Longfellow's writings or critical reception supports the assertion that he was a critic of American colonization—in fact, quite the contrary, as we have seen. And yet taken out of context, Longfellow's text at this point—the Native Americans' dutiful responses that they have listened to the missionary's words and will think about them—could easily support the ironic interpretation imputed to it. In other words, Hughes and Stradling are offering a presentist reading of the text, all but ignoring any historical basis for their interpretation. It is still far from obvious how Coleridge-Taylor's music facilitates their revisionist, critical rereading—in fact, its empathetic treatment of both parties seems to work mildly against this perspective. But reading historical colonial views ironically to anticolonial ends is one way to make the piece more palatable now. Longfellow's text—and Coleridge-Taylor's music by association—could be interpreted as ironic, if that makes them less awkward for us. There is just no evidence that this was their creators' intention, or that anyone understood the work in this way until the end of the twentieth century.

For all the nobility of Hiawatha's 'I am going, o my people' and the glorious swell of the final 'Farewell, farewell for ever'—and it is a moving and suitably thrilling conclusion to the three cantatas—the nostalgic sunset glow offers a comforting aesthetic sublimation of a human catastrophe. Hearing Coleridge-Taylor's most famous work now captures and amplifies these dissonances—not just of our own with an earlier age, but those that were already present at the time of its creation.

CHAPTER 5

IDENTITIES AND IDENTIFICATION

A HIAWATHAN OVERTURE

In 1899, with the success of *Hiawatha's Wedding Feast* already established and its sequel, *The Death of Minnehaha*, completed, Coleridge-Taylor penned an orchestra overture to Longfellow's epic. It was published as 'Overture to *The Song of Hiawatha*', and given the opus number 30, No. 3, in succession to the two existing pieces; the final cantata, *Hiawatha's Departure*, would become designated No. 4. Critical reactions were not quite as universally positive as those to the first two cantatas, and the overture has often been omitted in subsequent performances of the trilogy.[1] Nevertheless, it has not entirely disappeared, and recent performances suggest an attractive pendant to the more familiar trio of choral pieces on the subject, even if

Samuel Coleridge-Taylor's Hiawatha. Benedict Taylor, Oxford University Press.
© Oxford University Press 2025. DOI: 10.1093/oso/9780197649343.003.0005

the overture is perhaps not quite as memorable as some of Coleridge-Taylor's finest orchestral music—pieces like the Ballade in A minor, the later *Symphonic Variations on an African Air, Petite Suite de Concert,* or *Violin Concerto.*

Its opening gesture—a soulful rising phrase in the violins (see Ex. 5.1 below)—is suitably atmospheric with its glistening harp arpeggios and expressive violins doubled in octaves accompanying a deceptive harmonic progression, in which an initial plangent half-diminished B minor sonority falls via a diminished seventh to an unexpected D major tonic. Solo horn and oboe offer a nostalgic echo of the phrase, rooted now in the warmth of the major mode.

EX. 5.1   Coleridge-Taylor, *Hiawatha* Overture, primary thematic material and its final transformation into opening motive of *Hiawatha's Wedding Feast*

Again the progression is repeated; again the horn and oboe respond, the equivocation between minor and major creating a wistfulness and emotional ambiguity from the outset. On the third time, the descending sequence continues into a passage of sensuously slipping chromatic harmonies, redolent perhaps of Grieg (one of the composer's musical loves), major and minor vying for the upper hand amidst the rich seventh chords. At length, the music comes to rest on an expectant dominant. But this is not the dominant of D major, the key that was initially reached, but of the overture's opening sonority, B (whether major or minor is not yet determined). And after the briefest of pauses a sombre rhythmic pattern beats out solemn B minor chords, the accompaniment to the main theme of the ensuing sonata-form movement.

The theme that is heard here is transparently what the opening phrase had prefigured. But, more significantly, it also corresponds to a spiritual, 'Nobody knows the trouble I see, Lord', a fact hardly obscured by the metric reworking into triple time.[2] What is African American music doing here in a work based on purported Native Americans? Even in a piece reframed, as we saw in chapter 4, from as many different national perspectives as this, the introduction of a new group of peoples might come as a surprise. The link forged here between Native Americans and African Americans is indeed hardly self-evident, but as we will see, it is one that would play one of the most important roles in the spreading of Coleridge-Taylor's work and fame.

HIAWATHA'S HOMECOMING

The success of *Hiawatha* was not confined to Britain. Within a short time Coleridge-Taylor's cantatas would be exported to the land in which their story was set. As early as 23 March 1899—just four months after the London premiere—*Hiawatha's Wedding Feast* was presented in Brooklyn, New York, by the Temple Choir of Brooklyn. The complete cycle was given by the Albany Musical Association of New York in May 1901, and in the next three years there followed performances in Winstead (Connecticut), Easton (Pennsylvania), St Louis, Des Moines, Cleveland, Boston, and Nashville.[3] Such exposure made Coleridge-Taylor a talking point for white Americans, who readily took up the melodious setting of their own invented national epic by an English composer with no prior connection to their continent. But *Hiawatha*'s most notable impact, and where Coleridge-Taylor would leave his longest lasting legacy in the United States, would be on the nation's Black population. Coleridge-Taylor's example, of a Black figure who had achieved prodigious success and commanded respect from the prevailingly white musical world and society at large, was an enormous source of pride for African Americans. As Doris McGinty relates, 'While Americans in general were impressed by Samuel Coleridge-Taylor's success and intrigued by the thought that a person of African heritage could be the idol of London audiences, many African Americans looked upon the composer with an admiration that frequently bordered on hero worship.[4]

As early as 1900, the tenor solo 'Onaway! Awake' from the first cantata was performed in a concert by the Chicago

Symphony Orchestra under its founder, Theodore Thomas. As the Black weekly *The Freeman* reported, 'It is very probable that this was the first Negro's music that ever appeared on the program of the Thomas Orchestra. It was therefore an event of much interest to the American Negro.'[5] A front-page article in the Baltimore *Afro-American* of June 1903 conveys something of the excitement and hope which the emergence of Coleridge-Taylor to international celebrity held for Black Americans:

> The musical idol of London is a Negro.
> In the midst of the renewed effort on the part of thoughtful men and women in America to solve the great race question such an announcement almost challenges belief. But it is stating the true situation of which S. Coleridge Taylor is the central figure. . . . And not in England alone does this fame rest, for Coleridge Taylor's writings are known in America and valued here, too, for their great musical worth, a fact that was in evidence when the St Cecilia Society, one of the most famous musical organizations in this country, produced his greatest work, 'Hiawatha'.

This 'marvelous Negro', continues the author, 'has justified the claims of many of the great masters—that the Negro has innate musical genius and that it blossoms into melodic flowers whenever given the slightest encouragement'. Prophetically, it adds, 'It is said that he may soon visit America to personally direct some of his own works'.[6]

For indeed such was the clamour for the 'sweetest of musicians', this Black Chibiabos who had penned the music currently taking the English-speaking world by storm, that a group of prominent African Americans in the nation's capital decided to form a choral society, named in his honour, whose primary aim was to bring Coleridge-Taylor over to America to conduct them in his masterpiece. In all, Coleridge-Taylor visited the United States three times, in 1904, 1906, and 1910, on each occasion encountering significant success with Black and white populations alike. With *Hiawatha*, wrote the pioneering African American musicologist Ellsworth Janifer in 1967, Coleridge-Taylor 'proved to a race-conscious America, and to the world, that no one ethnic group held a monopoly upon musical genius. But more than this, his visits were a symbol of hope to aspiring Negro American composers struggling to assert their individuality in the face of almost insurmountable racial prejudice.'[7]

The idea of a 'Coleridge-Taylor Choral Society' arose towards the end of 1901 among some of the leading Black Washingtonians. These numbered many of the most prominent and affluent members of the city's sizeable African American population, who formed a social elite that was accustomed to 'performing' their respectability through participation in classical musical events, organized by the often highly educated and musically proficient women of this circle.[8] In their own account of the society's genesis, published in the programme to Coleridge-Taylor's first concerts with them:

> In a conference of our more prominent musicians, which met at the home of Mrs. A. F. Hilyer, it was discovered that the formation of a choral society among the colored singers of Washington had long been in the minds of many of them, and only needed the stimulus of the proposed visit of the composer

and the opportunity to sing 'Hiawatha' to give it tangible shape and permanent form. Its object is to develop a wider interest in the masterpieces of the great composers and especially to diffuse among the masses a higher musical culture and appreciation of works that tend to refine and elevate.[9]

News of the promising young Black British composer had been filtering through to African Americans via figures like Paul Laurence Dunbar, who had collaborated with Coleridge-Taylor back in 1898, and Frederick Loudin, director of the Fisk Jubilee Singers, who had toured London several times over the preceding decades and was a delegate alongside the composer at the inaugural Pan-African Conference held there in 1900. Put in touch by Loudin, Mamie Hilyer, a founding member of Washington's elite 'Treble Clef Club' choral society, had visited the composer in Croydon while travelling through Europe in 1900, and she brought her positive impression back to America. Following enthusiastic discussion, a friend of hers, Lola Johnson, wrote to Coleridge-Taylor in late 1901 extending an invitation to conduct his *Hiawatha*.[10] The composer was flattered by the offer and interested, but a combination of a busy schedule (in order to make ends meet his weeks were full with teaching, conducting, and adjudicating) and his demands for an adequate orchestra meant that it was not until the fall of 1904 that he arrived on the American continent.

In the meantime, preparations went ahead. Rehearsals started in 1901; the following year an 'S. Coleridge Taylor Day' was held to prepare and educate the public with talks and solo recitals devoted to the composer's music,[11] and by the spring of 1903 the 'S. Coleridge-Taylor Choral Society' were ready to put on their first concert, in the absence of the composer and with accompaniment provided by two pianists in place of an orchestra. On 23 April 1903, in the Metropolitan African Methodist Episcopal Church, Washington, the society gave their first rendition of *Hiawatha* to a packed and racially mixed audience. It was an overwhelming success. The white press came away having to reconsider their prejudices. 'Those who came expecting to make allowances for inadequate singing because it was by colored people went away wondering whether so effective a chorus had ever been heard in Washington', opined the *New York Times*, rather highmindedly. 'The concert opens up a field of interesting speculation as to the possibility of colored people in the higher regions of music.'[12] Adding to this account, *The Musical Times* in Britain reported back:

> The chorus-singing was really excellent and deserving of all praise. Even several eminent white musicians have borne testimony to its high achievement, and even the white press acknowledge that the performance was a splendid success. Considering the deep-rooted racial feeling among white and coloured people this is all the more gratifying and encouraging. Moreover we understand that it is the first time that white singers have applied in hundreds for admission to an entirely coloured Society (in U.S.A.) and have been refused admission because there was not room for them![13]

Two more performances followed, on 7 November 1903 (in Baltimore) and 12 April 1904, and by this time the *Washington Post* was in no doubt as to the level of accomplishment: 'We are prepared to say that there is not a finer chorus, nor a better trained one, in the United States'.[14]

Half a year later, the composer himself was standing on the podium to guide the society named after him in a series of three concerts making up a festival devoted to his music (see Fig. 5.1). For the first, held in Convention Hall, Washington, on 16 November 1904, *Hiawatha* was performed by the society with high-profile Black soloists including Harry Burleigh, the baritone who had sung spirituals to Dvořák in New York a decade earlier and a significant composer in his own right, and the Orchestra of the US Marine Corps. No Black orchestra could be found that seemed to offer the standard required, so the organizers engaged a white ensemble from the US military (proudly known as 'The President's Own', and once conducted by John Philip Sousa), which for the first time found itself under the command of a Black conductor. But they might have been better not to have bothered. While the Black press certainly remarked upon the substandard orchestral playing,[15] it was the white press that really laid into the players. The *Washington Post* was just one that observed how wretched the white, professional orchestra was ('at times inexcusably bad . . . ragged and amateurish'), and contrasted directly with the Black, amateur chorus ('magnificent from start to finish').[16] The result was no less a triumph for the society than for the composer and all those concerned with racial uplift in a divided United States.

Coleridge-Taylor's music and its performances provided a talking point for discussing what was styled the 'race problem' among both white and Black audiences. Even before the composer arrived, as we saw, the level of musical

The S. Coleridge-Taylor Choral Society

OF WASHINGTON, D. C.

ORGANIZED 1901. INCORPORATED 1903.

PROF. JOHN T. LAYTON, Musical Director.   MISS MARY L. EUROPE, Accompanist.

MUSICAL FESTIVAL

FOURTH RENDITION OF

S. COLERIDGE-TAYLOR'S

HIAWATHA

CONDUCTED BY THE COMPOSER.

SOLOISTS:

Mr. HARRY T. BURLEIGH, of New York, Barytone.

Mme. ESTELLA PINCKNEY CLOUGH, of Worcester, Mass., Soprano.

Mr. J. ARTHUR FREEMAN, of St. Louis, Tenor.

Accompanied by the Orchestra of the U. S. Marine Corps,
Lt. Wm. H. Santelman, Leader,

CONVENTION HALL,

Wednesday Evening, November 16th, 1904.

"CHORAL BALLADS" AND SELECTIONS,
Thursday Evening, November 17th.

"Hiawatha" at "The Lyric" in Baltimore, Friday Evening, Nov. 18

EIGHT O'CLOCK.

THE WEBER PIANO is kindly loaned by the courtesy of Mr. Percy S. Foster, Manager of Sanders & Stayman's, 1327 F St. N. W.

FIG. 5.1 Programme for the Coleridge-Taylor Festival put on by the
S. Coleridge-Taylor Choral Society of Washington, November 1904
(https://www.loc.gov/resource/lcrbmrp.t2604/)

attainment among African American executants was putting white performers to shame, and garnered attention in the white musical press. The *Washington Post* spoke of the brighter future the unanticipated success of the Coleridge-Taylor Choral Society held out; though the terms now seem excruciatingly patronizing, the possibilities of racial uplift presented were fully in keeping with the stated aims of the society:

> It is a generally recognized fact that the negro race is peculiarly gifted for song and instrumental music of a primitive order. This is because the great mass of them are, like the masses of all races, deprived of the higher opportunities. Given these, it is really marvelous to what a height of artistic excellence this people, but a generation removed from slavery, and not more than three or four from absolute savagery, can soar. In the contemplation of such facts it would seem that the solution of the race problem, in this country, were not so very distant, after all.[17]

The composer's own appearances on American soil galvanized public opinion. 'Visit of English Negro Composer Emphasizes American Prejudice' ran the headline of a *New York Times* editorial in November 1904, which used Coleridge-Taylor, and the success of the choral society named in his honour, as a stick with which to beat 'cocksure proponents of the "negro problem"', in other words, those proponents of white superiority. The author commented on the perceived differences between Coleridge-Taylor's treatment in his native England, where he was 'judged, not as a negro, but as a composer', and the contrasting situation for anyone comparable in the United States. What happened recently in Washington with the *Hiawatha* concert 'was rather curious for students of the many-sided and yet hitherto one-sided thing known as "the race problem"', for

> these colored people, by common consent and common admission, managed the Coleridge-Taylor festival better than anything in the musical line has been managed in Washington for years. The musical critics of the Washington papers, mostly Southerners, conceded that the chorus of Negroes was one of the best managed, best drilled, and most successful choruses that had ever appeared in Washington. The one weak point in the performance, according to critics, was the orchestra. And the orchestra, alone of the component parts of the festival, was made up of white men.[18]

The Black press hardly dissented from these views; indeed, favourable or sympathetic reports from the white press were sometimes directly reproduced in Black newspapers. Parts of the *New York Times*'s review of the first 1903 concert by the Coleridge-Taylor Choral Society, for instance, quoted above, were reprinted in the *Afro-American*'s own account of the performance, including the lines on those 'expecting to make allowances for inadequate singing because it was by colored people'.[19] It shared the white press's belief in the power of racial uplift through participation in respectable cultural activities, seeking acknowledgement and acceptance from white society in the terms set by the latter.[20] (Tellingly perhaps, on the same page as a report in the *Washington Bee* of a 1908 concert, which had concluded with satisfaction that 'many white citizens witnessed the performance, with evident enjoyment', were adverts for products to make 'colored skin' lighter.[21])

Not everyone was convinced, however, that for all the warm applause much had really changed for African Americans. It is conspicuous that the critical reflections in the white press were being made at a time when segregation laws were being passed across the country without much opposition being offered by these papers. And a more sceptical perspective was left by Anna Julia Cooper, the pioneering civil rights activist, who had met Coleridge-Taylor at the London Pan-African Conference in 1900 and been befriended by him and his wife. Cooper is an interesting figure here as a thinker whose views do not necessarily align with the mainstream Black press or the Black Washington elite:

> Mr. Taylor came alone to 'shed his sweetness' quite generously on 'colored' America. Some whites bravely attended the concert given in a 'colored' church. The Marine Band rehearsed faithfully under his baton and took orders quite meekly from the little brown Englishman. Not a ripple on the surface. The last goodbyes were said; colored Washington and neighboring boroughs were gloating over the triumph 'for the Race'.

And yet, 'Mr. White Man rarely gets left for long.'

> As a few of us learned afterwards, a committee . . . quietly boarded the train at Union Station, rode with Mr. Taylor as far as Philadelphia, bro[ugh]t him back as their guest, and banqueted him at the Shoreham! We were not invited.[22]

It had been Black Washingtonians who had invited and paid for Coleridge-Taylor's visit, but members of white society willingly reappropriated some of this glory. Looking back on events a decade later, an opinion piece in *The Freeman* entitled 'The Musical Progress of the Race' offered another mildly dissenting voice:

> Most of the concerts given by our people are either for show or for profit rather than for musical uplift. For the past sixteen years . . . I have noted that no one musical effort with simply the idea of presenting something 'big' has had any good after-effect . . . nor even the singing of Coleridge-Taylor's 'Hiawatha' has had any good after-effect. Probably because they have partaken of the rich dessert first and have no appetite for the nurishing [*sic*] things in the way of folk-songs and smaller progressive oratories.
>
> The race needs something much more than all it has had that we may educate the future fathers and mothers.[23]

If it rarely highlighted the displacement and devastation of the indigenous Americans, Coleridge-Taylor's *Hiawatha* had nonetheless made white America talk about its own race problem with those others it had displaced from another continent in order to serve them in slavery—and equally gave some African Americans new hope in overcoming it.[24] In this, *Hiawatha* could be co-opted by African American communities in the service of racial uplift—a cause that, as we will see, its composer certainly shared. Whether or not the desired social change was likely to be successful remained unclear.

SORROW SONGS

In his 1903 *The Souls of Black Folk*, the Black intellectual and activist W. E. B. Du Bois famously prefixes each chapter with a musical quotation of an African American spiritual;

no words are given, but the absent text associated with the melody tacitly informs the content of the following discussion. (Coleridge-Taylor had been sent Du Bois's book by Andrew Hilyer, treasurer of the S. Coleridge-Taylor Choral Society, early in 1904 before his visit to America, and described it as 'the greatest book he had ever read'.)[25] These 'sorrow songs', as Du Bois christens them, are ultimately brought to discussion in the final chapter, which forms an eloquent paeon to the music of the African Americans during their ordeal of slavery:

> Little of beauty has America given the world save the rude grandeur God himself stamped on her bosom. . . . And so by fateful chance the Negro folk-song—the rhythmic cry of the slave—stands to-day not simply as the sole American music, but as the most beautiful expression of human experience born this side the seas.[26]

Fortuitously, the very first 'sorrow song' in Du Bois's book is the similarly named—though musically quite distinct—'Nobody knows the trouble I've seen'. Although his overture was written four years before Du Bois's volume and can hardly have been influenced by it, there is something tantalizingly similar about the manner in which Coleridge-Taylor prefaces his trilogy with its own 'sorrow song', whose meaning in relation to the following three cantatas is not spelled out by the composer but requires—or so it appears—disentangling and interpretation by the listener or critic.

What does the presence of an African American spiritual in *Hiawatha* mean in this context? As said, the overture was written in 1899, several years before the composer's first visit to America and before any significant approach from African Americans, so it was not obviously written to flatter his future hosts. Coleridge-Taylor could have had little inkling that Black America would soon be taken over by 'Hiawatha-mania'.[27]

The version used in the overture differs from that Coleridge-Taylor could have found in *Jubilee Songs: As Sung by the Jubilee Singers*, edited by Theodore F. Seward and George L. White in 1872. 'Nobody knows the trouble I see, Lord' is the very first song in the songbook (Fig. 5.2).[28] Transposed down a semitone to B minor, Coleridge-Taylor's main theme (see Ex. 5.1) refashions each bar of the 2/4 original into two bars of 3/8 by softening the syncopations while preserving the short-long anapaest at the end of the second bar. His swinging triple rhythm imparts a possible folklike flavour with its 'Scotch snap' and modal colouring, though it is less openly African American in stylistic attributes. Only the opening 8-bar chorus is used by the composer, which through repetition, variation, and contrast with material that is nevertheless derived from it, is elaborated into a larger ternary first-theme group. The foreshadowing of this theme in the introduction also differs from the spiritual. Drawing just on the five pitches of the initial ascending phrase, although it retains the 2/4 time signature, this version is rhythmically simpler, with nothing of the characteristic syncopation, the dotted rhythm instead faintly march-like in suggestion.

The overture's opening equivocation between B minor and D major prefigures the ambiguity at the opening of the third cantata in the cycle, at that moment yet to be written, and we might wonder whether Coleridge-Taylor

FIG. 5.2 'Nobody knows the trouble I see, Lord', from *Jubilee Songs: As Sung by the Jubilee Singers* (1872)

was already thinking ahead to this concluding part to his series of cantatas. By providing a new potential starting point to the cycle, the composer encases the G major of *Hiawatha's Wedding Feast* and E minor of *The Death of Minnehaha* within the wider B minor/major frame given by the overture and *Hiawatha's Departure*. More pointedly, the final stages of the overture neatly set up the opening of *Hiawatha's Wedding Feast*, which now would follow.[29]

The main part of the overture is built as a sonata form in B minor, utilizing the 'Nobody knows' theme as first subject, and with secondary and closing material moving to the tonally distant keys of E flat and B flat major (another example of Coleridge-Taylor's love of semitonal relationships). Following a short development, in which the plainer introductory form of the spiritual's opening phrase is heard again (albeit modified into 3/8), a conventional recapitulation brings back the first and second themes in the tonic minor and major, respectively. Rather than leading directly to a close, though, the music lands on a preparatory dominant (b. 574/rehearsal 19), over which statements of the introductory motive provide an expectant buildup. The tension is released through the long-awaited cadence to the tonic B major (b. 590/rehearsal 20), initiating an *Allegro vivace* coda. Reverting to the introduction's 2/4 metre, at first the material heard here corresponds to the introductory form of the 'Nobody knows' motive, given *fortissimo* and in augmentation. But the melodic line now drops an octave from the upper F♯, and on its repetition the idea is transformed into an even simpler shape that retraces the rising fifth contour in repeated notes. This is nothing other than the very opening motive of *Hiawatha's Wedding Feast*, sounding as there in the trumpet, which has emerged seamlessly out of the first four notes of 'Nobody knows the trouble I see'. Though a cunning piece of motivic linkage, the opening idea of an African American spiritual has morphed before our ears into the start of Coleridge-Taylor's Native American cantata (illustrated in Ex. 5.1). Lest there be any doubt of the identity of the material now heard, this 'Gitchie Manito' motive (labelled *a* in chapter 3) is followed directly by the pentatonic-like continuation from the opening of the *Wedding Feast* (motive *b*). In the following bars the tonic is heard in alternation with the lowered submediant, G major—the opening key of *Hiawatha's Wedding Feast*, prepared here—while also prefiguring the end of the entire trilogy, the final moments of *Hiawatha's Departure* that lie in the future. Like those concluding bars, the final tonic harmony is approached by a plagal progression that touches in turn on the keys of the following three cantatas: G major, E minor, and finally B major.

This coda does more than simply prepare the opening sounds of the cantata that will follow at the overture's close: it fashions a link between two previously unconnected musical materials, associated with two ethnic groups that had apparently nothing in common. It calls attention to a possible analogy between—or even identification of—the two quite distinct peoples.

We recall from chapter 3 that Coleridge-Taylor's musical idol, Antonín Dvořák, had publicly claimed a few years earlier that he found the music of Native and African Americans to be practically indistinguishable, and that in several respects *Hiawatha's* musical idiom follows the model of Dvořák's American compositions. One straightforward explanation, then, is that Coleridge-Taylor was looking for characteristically 'American' material, and alighted on the spiritual, which, shorn of its syncopations, was pressed into service as standing more generally for an entire continent. Dvořák had after all asserted that the path to genuinely American music lay not in the culture of the white settlers but in the indigenous and Black populations. Dvořák's sentiments were echoed by the Black intellectual Booker T. Washington in his preface to Coleridge-Taylor's *Twenty-Four Negro Melodies* a few years later: 'The race as a whole realizes that apart from the music of the Red Man the Negro folk-song is the only distinctively American music, and is taking pride in using and preserving it.'[30] That African American and Native American cultures might be conflated is clearly questionable nowadays. Still, whether or not African American material is an appropriate stand-in for Native American music, there is no doubt that people at the time and even since—Black and white alike, if not perhaps Native American—perceived an affinity between the two groups that went beyond any purported musical similarities. McGinty points out that in contemporary accounts of performances of *Hiawatha*, 'The assumption that the black singers had a cultural identification with Native America and were therefore at an advantage singing this music was made more than once.'[31]

Still, we might expect Coleridge-Taylor to be more discriminating regarding matters of African American culture than the Bohemian Dvořák; he had already collaborated with Dunbar the previous year in exploring African and African American themes, and would surely have been aware that such a melody was not 'neutral' material.

Another possibility would be to see the fate of the Native Americans at the hands of the white American settlers mirrored in the struggles of the African Americans against the same white oppressors. Such a reading, common enough in the reception of Coleridge-Taylor's *Hiawatha*, links the two peoples owing to their common identification as victims. Even if there is no obvious criticism of American colonial expansion either in Longfellow or indeed Coleridge-Taylor's setting, a general sympathy for both groups was widespread in Britain in this period and commented upon in contemporary reviews.

In introducing the trilogy through a song associated with a specifically Christian belief in salvation, moreover, Coleridge-Taylor is relating his starting point to what forms the end point of Longfellow's epic tale in *Hiawatha's Departure*. More than simply a white narrative of the rise and decline of Native American culture, *The Song of Hiawatha* can be interpreted as an imaginative retelling of the coming of Christianity to the New World. It offers scant consolation perhaps to Native Americans. But given the central importance of Christianity for many African Americans in their ongoing struggle against political oppression and discrimination, *Hiawatha*'s culmination makes the poem less a tragedy and more a story of hope amidst misfortune. This point is explicitly made in an article on Coleridge-Taylor written just prior to his first visit in 1904, published in the Indianapolis weekly *The Freeman* (probably the closest the Black press had to a national newspaper at the time). For its author, W. Milton Lewis, Longfellow's poem tells of the 'childlike' and 'simple faith' of those 'children of the setting sun', such 'that we almost hate the fate that banished them to the "ends of the earth"'. Lewis reads the character of Hiawatha as an idealized, fictional hero, a Christlike or at least strongly Christian figure, his heart set upon establishing 'a new kingdom on earth'. Notably in this context he draws parallels with 'our own Booker T. Washington . . . an illustrious example of an Hiawatha; he advises his race to quit the internecine quarrels that it may grow stronger for the greater battle of life; pave the way to greater ease for the thousands of new-borns that they may escape misery-crowned days'. 'The Negroes of America can read Hiawatha with charm and profit', Lewis concludes: 'he is a most beautiful character; he breathed the sweeter blessings of peace—blessed peace—calm serenity; his object was to uplift mankind above carking care into the order of godhood'.[32]

As Du Bois had summed it up just a year before: 'What are these songs, and what do they mean? . . . They are the music of an unhappy people, of the children of disappointment; they tell of death and suffering and unvoiced longing toward a truer world, of misty wanderings and hidden ways.'[33] He is speaking of the 'sorrow songs', of course, but his words could conceivably apply to that other song—of Hiawatha.

THE SAVIOUR OF HIS PEOPLE

What has often been speculated upon is the extent to which Coleridge-Taylor himself—a fellow member of the African diaspora—not only sympathized but even identified with Longfellow's Native Americans in general, and Hiawatha in particular. Both during and after his lifetime it was commonplace to associate Coleridge-Taylor with the protagonist of his most famous work. On his gravestone in Bandon Hill Cemetery, near Croydon, a lengthy epitaph is completed by a musical quotation from the final scene of his trilogy: 'Thus departed Hiawatha/Hiawatha the beloved'. The English poet Alfred Noyes, who had collaborated with the composer on his last major choral work, *A Tale of Old Japan*, made the link foundational in his memorial poem eulogizing the composer. Noyes's conceit in his 'In Memoriam Samuel Coleridge-Taylor (September 3, 1912)' is to link an opening Longfellow-like vision of indigenous America (the allusion is to Hiawatha's departure to the isles of the blessed)

> *Farewell! The soft mists of the sunset sky,*
> *Slowly enfold his fading birch-canoe!*
> *Farewell! His dark, his desolate forests cry,*
> *Moved to their vast, their sorrowful depths anew*

with Coleridge-Taylor's homeland

> *Greater than England or than Earth discerned,*
> *He never paltered with this art for gain*

and the Africa of his paternal ancestry

> *Hear the strange grief that deepened through his own,*
> *The vast cry of a buried continent.*
> *Through his, his race a moment lifted up*
> *Forests of hands to Beauty as in prayer;*

in such a way that the purported primeval forests and primordial grief of Native America begin to blur with those of Africa. The 'lost world' that 'through him . . . hailed the light' in the final stanza is ambiguous: it could refer either to America or to Africa.[34] That someone might reflect in a eulogy on the composer's European and African heritage is unsurprising: but the addition of Native America to the mix shows just how closely Coleridge-Taylor had become bound to his youthful *magnum opus*. The English composer Havergal Brian was far from alone when he recalled Coleridge-Taylor as 'a man who was in all truth the image of the hero in his masterpiece, *Hiawatha*'.[35] The epithet 'the Hiawatha Man' does more than simply link the composer to the work that made him famous: it suggests a connection between the two heroes, one semi-fictional and Native American, one real and Anglo-African, both of whom were revered for their tireless work on behalf of their people and passed on to the next world all too early.[36]

Clearly Coleridge-Taylor's connection with *Hiawatha* went beyond the 'funny names' that he claimed initially drew him to the subject. On the morning of his marriage to Jessie Walmisley, 30 December 1899, Coleridge sent a touching telegram to his bride: 'I will never leave thee, dearest, I will take thee to my wigwam', signing it 'Hiawatha'.[37] And when their first child, a son, was born in 1900 the parents named him Hiawatha, an unusual choice one assumes for suburban England. The name reverberates with that of the father's recent professional triumph, but surely demonstrates a more personal affinity for Longfellow's character.

For some writers, Coleridge-Taylor's recourse to (fictional) Native American themes was part of a process of coming to terms with his own African identity. Geoffrey Self conjectures that 'possibly in his on-going process of identifying with the cause of his paternal race, he saw little distinction between the real plight of the one and the legendary or imaginary plight of the other'.[38] More expressly, Paul Richards sees the appeal of Longfellow's Indians as part of a strategy aimed at recovering his own absent father: 'Straining to catch his own unknown and distant father's voice, Coleridge-Taylor seems to have alighted at first on the Native American cadences in Longfellow.' Speaking explicitly of the overture to *Hiawatha*, Richards conjectures that 'by invoking an African-American spiritual (in a work ostensibly about Native Americans)', the composer was perhaps 'hoping to assist new audiences to see through the exoticism of Longfellow's poem to the wider social and political significance of the struggle for cultural and racial equality.'[39]

Certainly for many critics, Coleridge-Taylor's position, as someone marked as racially different in an age awash with racially essentialized theorizing, is assumed to have given him an intrinsic empathy with another oppressed group of peoples. Coleridge-Taylor was partly African, partly British, by ancestry, and Africa was at this very period at the peak of its colonial domination by European powers (Britain foremost among them); he was constantly subjected to low-level but nevertheless unpleasant racial abuse in his day-to-day life; and therefore, so it is argued, he was more aware than most white European or American contemporaries about the dangers and sorrows of colonial exploitation, whether this involved American settlers or British imperial expansion.

Whether Coleridge-Taylor actually thought along these lines is not easy to establish. Quite evidently, he was certainly proud of his African heritage and became strongly committed to the cause of Black uplift in just the period he wrote his cantatas. Evidence for this is legion and need not be restated here.[40] Equally, his opposition to the historical blight of slavery is not in dispute. Whether or not this meant rejection of, or even marked criticism of, historical and ongoing American (and British) colonial activity is much less clear.[41] There is abundant scholarship to show that being Black and British in the early twentieth century did not necessarily entail a complete rejection of empire; rather, there were a variety of possible positions between accommodation, desire for a more equal commonwealth of nations, aspiration for independence as an inevitable but future state, and outright rejection.[42] Moreover, it is arguable that even quite radical Black thinkers in Europe and North America were still viewing their aspirations for social rights, political equality, and self-determination through a more-or-less white frame of reference (recent scholars have in fact claimed that many of the progressive delegates at the 1900 Pan-African conference that Coleridge-Taylor attended espoused views that would seem racist by today's standards).[43] And while plenty of composers have seen their art as engaging with political struggles, critics and scholars are arguably even more inclined to indulge in such readings.

Coleridge-Taylor's own sense of 'identity'—the precise nature of his relation to his African heritage vis-à-vis his English ancestry and upbringing, as well as the extent this marked his music—is contested and by no means uncontroversial. Attempting to understand the beliefs and background assumptions of a previous age is difficult enough at the best of times, let alone in a situation in which racial inequalities are rife. Most of the accounts left of the composer are by white commentators and friends, but there appears to have been a significant circle of West African friends known to him in London, of and from which rather less is known. While the composer's own daughter, Avril (Gwendolen) 'had no doubt that he thought of himself as an Englishman', in his relationships with African American friends and colleagues Coleridge-Taylor could manifest what appears to be an African diasporic identity. The two allegiances need not be mutually exclusive, of course. Personal identity may often be better understood not as something fixed or immutable but relational and negotiated with those around the subject, to this extent somewhat 'performative' in nature. How it is construed depends on who is asking, on the needs of those writing history.[44]

In her biographical sketch of her late husband, Coleridge-Taylor's widow, Jessie, relates one of his last remarks as he lay in bed with the pneumonia that was very shortly to claim him: 'When I die, the critics will call me a Creole'—'this, because Coleridge was always amused at the varied nationalities to which the critics considered he belonged' she explains.[45] This is how his wife interpreted the line. Inevitably, other commentators interpret it differently. While Paul Richards sees the remark as arising more out of worry than amusement—from the composer's fear of his music being essentialized in terms of his mixed racial origins—others come down firmly on one side or the other.[46] William Tortolano simply asserts that it shows 'he wanted to be a Negro musician'.[47] Sidney Butterworth disagrees entirely with this idea, though, claiming that being cast as a 'black' composer' was something 'he so earnestly hoped to avoid'.[48]

Berwick Sayers reports that Coleridge-Taylor soon tired of reviewers reading his race into his music and made clear that he was 'a British musician' and wanted to be valued for his music, not simply as a representative of 'negro music'.[49] Despite this apparent wish, critics have persisted doing just what the composer seems to have feared. The different responses to the composer's dying remark foregrounds the issue of how to interpret his identity. And ironically, Coleridge-Taylor's original remark was about interpretations of his identity.

The meaning of the term 'Creole', however, is mobile and fluid; it has meant different things for different places and times. In recent years, at least, the concept of creolization has become regarded more positively, holding that linguistic and cultural fusion is a fundamental part of most creativity, and its interpretative flexibility has been seen as an advantage. Indeed, contrary to the composer's remark, Richards has suggested that the epithet 'Creole' is not ill-chosen.[50] Coleridge-Taylor was in more than one a sense a Creole: not only mixed race, but a Sierra Leonean *Krio* on his father's side. His most famous creation, *Hiawatha*, encapsulates a heady mix of different identities, and its reception displays a still more bewildering constellation of identifications. On the one hand, put in negative terms, the source text and to some extent even the music are almost bursting with various forms of appropriation, questionable identities, and cultural differences that are passed over unheeded. On the other, the imaginative inhabitation of other standpoints is arguably a condition for the very possibility of empathy with other peoples, and some of *Hiawatha*'s curious cultural melange could be understood more positively as itself a type of creolization.

The distinguished Nigerian composer Akin Euba (1935–2020), in a review of a study of Coleridge-Taylor's music, proposed understanding his predecessor's output from the perspective of what he termed 'interculturalism'. (Like Euba, in fact, Coleridge-Taylor's African heritage was Nigerian-Yoruba, from his paternal grandfather, John Taylor.) Interculturalism for Euba is a positive force, manifested in Coleridge-Taylor's music by his 'blending Western elements with African and African American elements; indeed, his position as an intercultural composer is strengthened by his use of Native American elements in the *Hiawatha* trilogy'.[51] The distinction between cultural appropriation and interculturalism can be a fine one; it rests on interpretation.

CHAPTER 6

AFTERLIVES

DANCE FOR US YOUR MERRY DANCES

When Coleridge-Taylor died suddenly on 1 September 1912—pneumonia on top of overwork bringing about an untimely end when he was just thirty-seven years of age—he left unfinished his final contribution to the *Hiawatha* story: a ballet. The tale that had accompanied him from his college days through unforeseen success and worldwide celebrity fittingly marked his last work. A short score was left; nine of its dances were arranged and orchestrated by Percy E. Fletcher and published in two suites, the first in 1919 and the second (as *Minnehaha*) in 1925 (see Fig 6.1, a and b). As originally conceived, the ballet was an independent work unrelated to the three cantatas; there are no thematic links between the two, even though it goes over

Samuel Coleridge-Taylor's Hiawatha. Benedict Taylor, Oxford University Press.
© Oxford University Press 2025. DOI: 10.1093/oso/9780197649343.003.0006

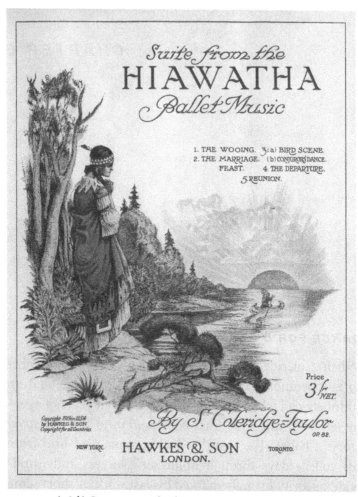

FIG. 6.1 (a & b) Cover pictures for the two *Hiawatha* Ballet Suites, Op. 82

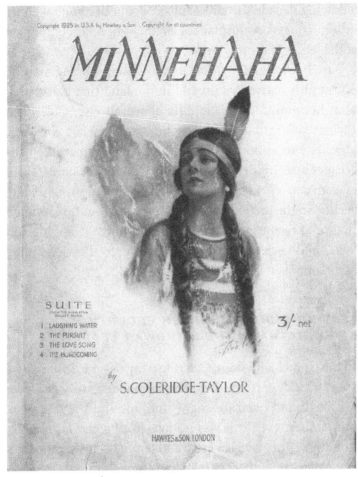

FIG. 6.1 Continued

several of the same scenes (these are, namely, 'The Wooing' from canto X, not set in the earlier cantatas; the familiar trio of 'Hiawatha's Wedding Feast', 'The Famine', and 'Hiawatha's Departure'; and a final 'Reunion in the Land of the Hereafter' added to Longfellow's story).[1] But in the following decade the ballet music would become taken up in semi-staged performances as an additional component of the larger *Hiawatha* cycle. For *Hiawatha* did outlive its composer by some margin. Both in his native Britain and in the land that had wooed him, his music, and *Hiawatha* above all else, Coleridge-Taylor's music remained a significant presence for some time. His reception in Britain and North America in the decades after his death shows something of the political climate in each. And his recent revival, following a significant decline in the second half of the twentieth century, offers a chance to reconsider his life, legacy, and the changing aesthetic and societal factors contributing to the vicissitudes in fortune seen in his most famous work.

PLAYING INDIANS: BRITISH RECEPTION OF HIAWATHA *IN THE INTERWAR YEARS*

In the United Kingdom, Coleridge-Taylor's music remained an intrinsic part of the performing canon—what people liked (and liked to sing)—until around the middle of the century, even if it was no longer critically fashionable to admire this music. First and foremost was inevitably *Hiawatha*, though some of the composer's other pieces also kept a place in repertories, such as the *Petite Suite de Concert*, Op. 77 (1911), whose exquisite second movement, 'Demand et Réponse', remained familiar for some time. If not quite reaching the mania of the first decade of the century, *Hiawatha* still proved a regular fixture for choral societies up and down the country, and sales of vocal scores helped keep Coleridge-Taylor's publisher Novello's in good financial health (second-hand copies from this time are still readily available).

The most spectacular sign of *Hiawatha*'s continued currency in its composer's homeland were the annual stagings of the trilogy as a type of musical pageant, held by the Royal Choral Society (RCS) in London's Royal Albert Hall from 1924 to 1939. The society had originally commissioned *Hiawatha's Departure* back in 1900 and had proudly programmed the trilogy almost every year since. Fourteen seasons were given under the canny direction of the producer Thomas Charles Fairbairn, who had been in discussion with the composer about a dramatization of the work shortly before the latter's death.[2] Some of the music from the unfinished ballet was incorporated into the course of the three cantatas, being called upon for Pau-Puk Keewis's dances towards the end of *Hiawatha's Wedding Feast* (Act 1), and a 'Ballet of Spring' at the start of Act 3 (*Hiawatha's Departure*). The musical arrangement was undertaken by the composer's son, Hiawatha Coleridge-Taylor, who conducted these parts of the show in the first season.

Eight performances were initially put on in May 1924 as a charitable event in aid of the Royal National Institute for the Blind; these proved so popular that Fairbairn decided to book the hall out for a fortnight the following year, with similar success. After a two-year hiatus the series resumed in 1928; thereafter, until the outbreak of the Second World War put a stop to the revelry, every June crowds in their thousands would descend on the Royal Albert Hall, many attired in 'Red Indian' costumes. A chorus of 800, all dressed in appropriate 'exotic' garb, and 200 dancers allowed the promoters to make a selling point of the thousand 'Indians' to be seen. Photographs show an enormous painted backcloth, wigwams on stage, and a real waterfall that drained down into an existing stream running under the hall (see Fig. 6.2). The show also brought the attraction of a real 'Red Indian': the Mohawk Chief Os-Ke-Non-Ton, a native Canadian who played the role of the medicine man introduced into the production. Malcolm Sargent (1895–1967), conductor of the RCS from this period onwards, directed nearly every season and became indelibly associated with Coleridge-Taylor's work.[3] Recordings of the first two cantatas made at this time by Sargent and the Royal Choral Society, both slightly abridged, give a fascinating flavour of the occasion: they are marked by an enthusiasm, sincerity,

FIG. 6.2   Stage set for *Hiawatha*, Act 1, Royal Albert Hall, interwar period. Chief Os-Ke-Non-Ton is performing as the Medicine Man. The Museum of Music History

and pathos as well as a degree of technical imprecision quite foreign to modern performing style.[4]

The Royal Choral Society were an amateur group, so costs were kept low, and with their numbers so high they ensured that plenty of family and friends would be in the audience. The colour and spectacle brought to vivid life the glamour of the American West familiar from black and white movies. The production was popular among families and children, who would often come dressed for the part, many of whom were exposed to Coleridge-Taylor's music in this manner. Capitalizing on this potential audience, Novello's issued an arrangement of *Hiawatha's Wedding Feast* for higher voices (S.S.A.A) in 1934 (Fig. 6.3): advertised for 'female or boys' voices', it was explicitly designated as being 'Suitable for School performances'.[5] (Paralleling the fate of Longfellow's poetry at the time, the association with women and children probably did not help *Hiawatha* to be valued as part of a hard-nosed twentieth-century canon.)

The outbreak of the Second World War put a stop to the festivities; thereafter a solitary revival of the format was made in Coronation Year of 1953, albeit with different musical forces.[6] A projected repeat performance at the Proms the following year was cancelled owing to poor ticket sales, though the Society's regular concert renditions of the trilogy under Sargent continued for several more years. While critics still acknowledged the 'simplicity' and 'spontaneous sincerity' of the music, it was now sounding inescapably dated to post-war ears, and the time for fancy dress had passed.

For all those concerned at the time, the pageant doubtless appeared innocent escapism and provided an imagined

FIG. 6.3 Cover for the children's version of *Hiawatha's Wedding Feast*, Novello's vocal score issued in 1934

link with the romance and the tragedy of a people that had all but been wiped off the map. As Nicholas Cook sums it up, "The massed choral performances of the "Hiawatha" trilogy afforded their amateur participants a surrogate experience of indigeneity, the thrill of identification with an exotic other.[7] Nowadays critical indignation would be off the scale at the unashamed cultural appropriation of it all, in which the problems already foundational in Longfellow's poem and hardly circumvented in Coleridge-Taylor's setting are manifested for all to see (the visual spectacle and participatory element indeed performs them more plainly, more effectively than words or music alone). It is arguable in this sense whether the colonial appropriation is really any worse in the stage show than in the poem or music; it is just more obvious. What is further noteworthy here is how the material was reframed yet again for a new audience, to serve a fresh set of aims. The synopsis for the show, written by the critic Robin H. Legge, frames the 'opera' (as he calls it) in terms of Christian imagery and contemporary British imperial pride, the latter an unexpected and intriguing counterpart to the American colonial subtext seemingly so intrinsic to the poem. To achieve the latter, Legge performs a sleight of hand with the potential ambiguity resulting from Longfellow's conflation of the Iroquois Hiawatha with the Ojibwe Manabozho, and the extension of these native lands over present-day Canada:

> To understand the story it is necessary to know that it had been revealed to the Indian tribes by Gitche Manito, the Great Spirit and Creator of all living things, that he would send to them from the land where there is no sin and no darkness, and

where all is bathed in the glory of light and love, a great prophet who would teach them to adore the beauty of peace and who, after suffering with them the sorrows and privations of mankind, would lead them into the golden dawn of a new world.

In the fulness of time, Hiawatha was born, and became a great prophet, teacher and stateman. Under his influence five adjacent tribes buried the hatchet and wedded themselves together as a powerful confederation which became allied to the British settlers and fought besides them against the Hurons and their allies, the French. Thus, Hiawatha played a considerable part in the history of the formation of the British Empire, in that he assisted to a great extent in the acquisition of Canada.[8]

Already within its composer's lifetime a performance of *The Death of Minnehaha* in York had been put on with 'action and scenic effects', framed by a new spoken prologue and concluding tableau that explicitly framed the story in terms of its ultimate Christian message—'the idea being to illustrate the dawn of Christianity in North America'.[9] Whereas in 1910 tribute was paid to the work of early European missionaries, by 1925 national pride and worldly empire are also at stake. In Legge's statement that the 'White Race— traders, settlers and missionaries—[are] bringing to the depths of the virgin forest civilisation and the Faith and Hope of Christianity', there is little hint that any subversive anticolonial messages were perceived.

BUILDING A BLACK CANON: HIAWATHA IN NORTH AMERICA

If *Hiawatha* was utilized in Britain for essentially escapist entertainment, over the Atlantic in the same period it was playing a more frequent part in an overtly political cause, one that had been dear to its composer. The S. Coleridge-Taylor Choral Society of Washington gradually decreased its activities in the years after its namesake's second and last visit to conduct them in 1906. (His 1910 trip was to New England and did not include a journey to Washington to see his friends there.) As McGinty suggests, the society had fulfilled its primary purpose, and by the following decade several of its important members were getting on in years and decided to lay down their lances.[10] There were still plenty of performances of the cantatas in the 1920s among both white and Black choral societies across the country. The choral society of Howard University—the historically Black college at which Coleridge-Taylor had given a special lecture on 'Folklore Melodies of the Negro Race' back in 1906—presented the entire trilogy in Baltimore and Washington in April 1920.[11] Baltimore saw the work again in 1926, this time under the baton of W. Llewellyn Wilson, director of music at Frederick Douglass High School and a long-standing advocate of this music, while the Coleridge-Taylor Choral Society, still alive and singing, performed it back at the Metropolitan A.M.E Church in Washington in May 1927, the site of their most spectacular success over two decades earlier, and again a year later as part of the Sixteenth Convention of the National Association of Colored Women's Clubs in Washington.[12] More common were performances of individual cantatas, *Hiawatha's Wedding Feast* being most popular: it was given for instance at Whittier College, California, in 1921, at Taylor University (alongside *The Death of Minnehaha*) and St. Cloud State in 1926. The Minneapolis Symphony

Orchestra and Schola Cantorum of Lawrence College, meanwhile, put on *Hiawatha's Departure* in 1927. In 1920, New York saw a staged production of the *Wedding Feast*, complete with Native American dancers and 'Indian' dress, showing that the appeal of the work as exotic spectacle in America was just as strong as it soon became in Britain.[13]

In 1932 the famous African American tenor Roland Hayes sang Chibiabos in a Maine Festival performance of the *Wedding Feast*. That same year the composer's sacred cantata *The Atonement*—one of the items he had conducted in America in 1906—was sung in the Metropolitan A.M.E. Church in Washington. But whether through changing tides and tastes or as a result of the Depression years, performances started falling off in the United States during the 1930s, rather sooner than was the case in Britain. The significant exception to the decline in Coleridge-Taylor's fortunes was within African American communities, where the composer was still reckoned a crucial figure for his role in the development of Black cultural identity in the realm of classical music. Performances of the *Wedding Feast* persisted in places like Virginia State College (1931) and Tuskegee Institute (1937), and in 1938 the Music Club of Lincoln University, Pennsylvania, formed their own 'Coleridge-Taylor Choral Society' to perform their namesake's most famous creation.[14] Occasional performances of *Hiawatha* continued in Historically Black Colleges and Universities well into the middle of the century.[15] By 1966, however, a reviewer in the *Afro-American* could comment 'Samuel Coleridge-Taylor's name is relatively unknown in America except to a few choral groups and musicians who perhaps perform his cantata "Hiawatha's Wedding Feast" or sing some of his songs or play his organ works.'[16] When Columbia Masterworks brought out their pioneering 'Black Composers' series in 1974, Coleridge-Taylor, featured on the second volume, would inevitably be represented by 'Onaway! Awake'; but by then his music clearly belonged to a distant age, ripe for rediscovery as a historical curiosity.[17]

Nevertheless, in the decades after his death Coleridge-Taylor became incorporated into a 'Black Classical Canon' promulgated by aspirational Black communities in important centres like Chicago and Harlem.[18] A year after his death, a music school was opened in Chicago that was named after him; one of its pupils in the 1920s was Margaret Bonds (her mother in fact taught at the school), who would later become one of the first African American composers to achieve national prominence. This example is moreover far from unique: numerous Black schools and institutions would take their name after Coleridge-Taylor in this period. His music was still popular, even if performances of *Hiawatha* were less the focus than before, but it was his exemplary status as a figure who had commanded the respect of the white musical world and even been honoured by an audience with a US president that ensured Coleridge-Taylor's remaining a foundational figure for African Americans. His life and achievement were accordingly readily mobilized in the cause of Black uplift. A good example is a 1946 publication *Rising Above Color* that presents a series of inspiring pen portraits of otherwise entirely Black American figures.[19] 'Only a small number of our own list of distinguished Negro personalities could be included in this volume' writes the editor, Philip Henry Lotz of the thirteen figures chosen. 'They are truly among America's great.'[20] What he fails to note is that Coleridge-Taylor was not actually American. In the fifth chapter, 'Samuel Coleridge-Taylor, Musician', a brief account of the composer's life (with information mainly drawn from Sayer's biography) is followed by a series of pedagogical 'Questions for Discussion'. The latter—questions like 'What distinctive contribution to music has come from Africa? Is there a difference between African and American Negro music?'; 'What is the difference between "ragtime" and "jazz"?'—are about African and African American issues and have little if any direct relation to the preceding account of Coleridge-Taylor, even if it is fair to assume the composer would have been in complete sympathy with the book's underlying aim of racial uplift.[21]

Indeed, if Coleridge-Taylor was written out of (white) histories of the English Musical Renaissance over the course of the twentieth century, he was incorporated into Black American narratives, to the extent that he becomes a virtual (African) American. When Janifer, writing in 1967 about the composer's first concert in Washington, claims, 'Never did a composer receive a more tumultuous ovation from his own people!', he is no doubt appealing to the common African ancestry and sense of transnational, 'Black Atlantic' identity shared between Coleridge-Taylor and Washington's African American community.[22] But when a Black American newspaper ran an account of *Hiawatha*'s early success under the headline 'An Afro-American Musical Genius', a change of nationality had clearly been effected.[23] (This is the same composer who retorted 'I am an Englishman!' to white racist hecklers on a train in America.)[24]

This desire to lay claim to the composer may partly explain a story propagated at present (appearing as an unsourced claim on Wikipedia and repeated in several places) that Coleridge-Taylor was descended from African American slaves ('Black Loyalists') who had sided with the British during the American Revolution in exchange for freedom—in other words, had an ancestral link to America.[25] This seems unlikely, and no source that I have found suggests any basis for the story; it does not appear to originate from the composer's own time. Indeed, what we know of the composer's paternal line argues rather that his grandfather, John Taylor, originated in Ilawo in Nigeria, where his Egba people, displaced during the Yoruba wars of the 1820s, were all-too-easily preyed upon by slave traders, and was likely a 'recaptive' from a slave ship intercepted en route to the Americas by the Royal Navy and brought back to Sierra Leone where the British had established a colony for freed and recaptive slaves.[26] Of his paternal grandmother nothing seems to be known. But repetition of the 'Black Loyalist' story suggests that later audiences wanted to believe there were closer links between the United States and the composer than in all likelihood existed. Equally, the identification of Coleridge-Taylor with African American concerns is such that it is not unheard of for commentators even in Britain to assume mistakenly he was American.

TO THE LAND OF THE HEREAFTER

The second half of the twentieth century saw a precipitous decline in Coleridge-Taylor's standing amongst the predominantly white classical musical cultures of Britain and the United States. For years, except in specific Black cultural circles in America, he had been ignored by critical canons, for whom Victorian and Edwardian music as a whole was suspect, and Coleridge-Taylor's compositions in particular were simply too accessible, too pleasant, not progressive or angsty enough to take seriously. The composer could not even be claimed to have initiated any school or larger trend in British music, unlike his elders at the RCM, Stanford and Parry, or fellow student Vaughan Williams. As a consequence, accounts of the so-called English Musical Renaissance from this time ignore him entirely. By the 1960s and '70s, Coleridge-Taylor does not even warrant a mention in histories of classical musical composition in Britain from the late nineteenth to mid-twentieth centuries.[27] But even the place of *Hiawatha* in the performing repertory of choral societies was falling away (unlike, to this extent, the otherwise partly comparable case of Arthur Sullivan, whose comic operas written with W. S. Gilbert were even more critically maligned and omitted from the historiography of the 'Musical Renaissance', but still popular among middlebrow music lovers and amateur performers throughout the century). As we saw, attempts to bring back the staged productions of *Hiawatha* at the Royal Albert Hall wilted after 1953, and by the 1960s choral societies were losing interest. A 1975 performance of the three cantatas in Croydon to mark the centenary of the composer's birth, broadcast by the BBC, was something of a rarity.[28] The conductor of that commemorative performance, Kenneth Alwyn, would go on to record the trilogy in 1991 with the forces of the Welsh National Opera for the Argo (Decca) label, but that remains the only complete commercial recording to this day. Sir Malcolm Sargent's fine 1962 *Wedding Feast* has been in and out of the catalogue, but his earlier 1930s recordings of this and *The Death of Minnehaha* were never reissued from the original 78 rpm gramophone records. Even as late as 2013, when the Three Choirs Festival, held in Gloucester, revived the trilogy, critics' responses were mixed. Admitting the 'attractive fluency of the music' and 'its expertly deft scoring', Andrew Clements in *The Guardian* nevertheless found the cantatas lacking 'any real sense of dramatic pacing or vivid characterisation.'[29] It seems not to have occurred to people a century earlier that dramatic pacing would be at issue for an unstaged choral work; if anything *Hiawatha* was thought as demonstrating considerably more dramatic flair than contemporary cantatas. Such are our changing expectations and aesthetic demands.

As suggested above, the eclipse of Coleridge-Taylor and *Hiawatha* needs to be seen in the broader context of a decline in interest in Victorian and Edwardian music in general since the First World War, and especially the decline of the participatory choral culture that supported *Hiawatha*'s persistence in the amateur repertory well into the middle of the century. The middle-class choral societies that sustained *Hiawatha* still exist, but as a long waning institution stretching back to the nineteenth century. Another aspect of Coleridge-Taylor's output relevant to this discussion involves its proximity to the (admittedly disputed) concept of 'light music'. Although the composer himself seems not to have been especially drawn to this aesthetic,[30] his music's general stylistic characteristics are not too distant from those commonly associated with this category now, and it is eminently possible to hear works like the *Petite Suite de Concert*, his incidental music to stage plays like *Othello* and *Nero*, or indeed the surviving *Hiawatha* ballet as 'light music' of the highest quality. Either way, his melodically appealing, adeptly scored, expertly crafted, accessible compositions, never threatening to push the boundaries of contemporary musical style too far, hardly fit into a conventional modernist narrative of musical progress. In this, his declining reputation might be compared with that of a near contemporary like Edward German, who likewise displayed impeccable credentials as a symphonic composer but became known for light opera and tuneful incidental music.

No judgement about value is implied here in my use of the term 'light music', but historically there was often a comparison, stated or unstated, with music of apparently greater seriousness, 'depth' or 'profundity' (the scare quotes around all these terms show their awkwardness; the fact that I still employ them testifies to their utility). And it is clear, for instance, in early reviews, that Coleridge-Taylor's initial success with *Hiawatha* was expected to lead to even greater—or deeper, or more progressive—works. 'To be sure, it is all very simple and natural and not at all "profound"' wrote an early review—one that otherwise appears unstinting in praise. 'But if "Hiawatha's Wedding-Feast" cannot perhaps be called a great work, these simple and natural outpourings of our young friend are prophetic of great things in the future.'[31] Underlying this appeal to 'greatness' is a valorization of an idea of depth that likely stems from German Romantic musical aesthetics. Elgar, for instance, also wrote plenty of excellent 'lighter' music, but in the following decade he would become acclaimed internationally for his oratorios, symphonies, and concertos. A convenient coincidence can serve as an instructive example. At the Birmingham Festival in October 1900, August Jaeger, hoping to advance the careers of the two most promising English composers on his books at Novello, invited two influential German colleagues to attend two major choral concerts on the same day: the world premiere of *The Dream of Gerontius* in the morning and the second performance of the complete *Hiawatha* trilogy in the evening. The performances ranged from shambolic to barely adequate; the public and critics were enthusiastic about both (contrary to popular legend) but took to *Hiawatha* rather more readily. Elgar's work, an account of a dying man and his soul's journey following death, was unmistakably Roman Catholic and as such a little suspect in Protestant England; moreover, it appeared too demanding for even the best choirs. Conversely, Coleridge-Taylor's colourful 'Indian Legend' was taken up by choral societies throughout the country. But it was *Gerontius*, not *Hiawatha*, that was chosen to be taken back to Germany, where its triumphant performances led to Richard Strauss's celebrated proclamation of Elgar as the 'first English progressive musician'.[32] Rightly or wrongly, *Hiawatha* was always seen as attractive, melodious, accessible, and ultimately middlebrow. It rarely fully won over those critics seeking either profundity or progress.

The extent to which Coleridge-Taylor's mixed-race background—or rather perceptions of it—impacted the above considerations is open to debate. It is worth considering whether a white composer with similar musical talents and characteristics would not have suffered a similar eclipse in the twentieth century for precisely the reasons above.[33] This would by itself offer a sufficient reason for the decline in *Hiawatha*'s standing over the century, though in Coleridge-Taylor's case his unusual mixed-race background would have further placed him on the margins of any white-centred narrative of British music and, in conjunction with the datedness of *Hiawatha*'s subject matter, served to sideline him from serious critical consideration. Yet now, conversely, the remarkable story of the mixed-race musician from late-Victorian England that had the musical world at his feet is serving to open up Coleridge-Taylor's work once again, and modern-day listeners are rediscovering how wonderfully appealing and skilfully wrought so much of his music is.

It was Akin Euba who, in a spirit of optimism, predicted in 2001 that 'there could well be a Coleridge-Taylor resurgence in the near future.' 'Today, neo-African art music and intercultural music enjoy strong constituencies and, therefore, Coleridge-Taylor is no longer the isolated figure that he was in his lifetime.'[34] The last few years have indeed witnessed an explosion of interest in Coleridge-Taylor in Britain, his music suddenly having become a frequent fixture in concert and broadcasts. And yet the current revival in interest in the composer seems less about *Hiawatha* and the choral music than his chamber and orchestral music (with some piano music and songs included for good measure). While the chamber works of his student years are regularly encountered now, those choral works that were major successes in his lifetime like *A Tale of Old Japan* are nowhere to be seen, and even *Hiawatha* is honoured more in name than performance. Though the *Fantasiestücke* or

Nonet, the *Negro Melodies*, and Violin Concerto may well crop up in concert halls or on the radio, one searches in vain for *The Atonement* or *Meg Blaine*.

Much of this is surely due to the change in how the musical public receives music: in his lifetime a significant degree of exposure to Coleridge-Taylor's music was through participation in performance, favouring accessible works for choir or other forms of amateur music making. With a shift in performing culture, people now experience music primarily as auditors, through recordings and to a lesser extent concert attendance. The result is that the contemporary Coleridge-Taylor revival is actually revealing a quite different side of the composer's output, minimizing the big choral works with their Victorian and Edwardian ethos and concentrating much more on his instrumental music. No longer the 'Hiawatha Man', Coleridge-Taylor is stepping out of the shadow of his most famous work. Ironically, too, a book which started out discussing the uncertain canonical status of *Hiawatha* is now more about the growing canonical status of Coleridge-Taylor and his other music. But this also means that the politically questionable aspects of *Hiawatha*'s story may prove less of a concern: while Coleridge-Taylor is suddenly more fashionable, *Hiawatha's Departure* seldom gets an airing to trouble consciences. An image of Coleridge-Taylor built around his instrumental music distances him from aspects of his contemporaneous culture, manifested rather more evidently in *Hiawatha*, that we might prefer not to associate with him, hence making it easier to construct a heroic narrative around the composer as an artist who was ahead of his time in espousing something closer to our own progressive values.

What does this tale of *Hiawatha* hold, then, for attempts to understand both the past and our own present age? And what are the challenges that Coleridge-Taylor's most famous work poses for the modern concept of a canon? As has been apparent since the opening chapter, the variance in esteem for Coleridge-Taylor and his work problematize the idea that there is either a single 'canon' or that composers of colour were necessarily marginalized in the past. The fact that Britain at the height of Empire could embrace Coleridge-Taylor and its people take his music to their hearts does not of course absolve the age of culpability in activities that seem to many of us deeply regrettable. Neither does it lessen the questionable elements within that contemporaneous popularity—the racial essentializing that lies under the surface in much criticism of the time. But the very fact that this could once have been the case might serve as a reminder that the past is indeed a foreign country (L. P. Hartley's well-known apothegm is indeed singularly apt for a product of the year 1900), and people did indeed do things differently then from how we might now assume they did. *Hiawatha*'s early reception holds a potential cautionary tale for a contemporary age which likes to signal its own virtue by calling out others without looking at the nuances of the case, or without putting itself into another culture and mindset, as far as we can reconstruct it. More positively, it might also serve as a source of renewed inspiration—that many seemingly unlikely things are possible—for they were back then.

NOTES

CHAPTER 1

1   W. C. Berwick Sayers, *Samuel Coleridge-Taylor, Musician: His Life and Letters* (London: Cassell, 1915, rev. ed. Augener, 1927), pp. 58, 59.

2   Arthur Jacobs, *Arthur Sullivan: A Victorian Musician*, 2nd edition (Aldershot: Scolar Press, 1992), p. 390.

3   'Samuel Coleridge-Taylor. Born August 15, 1875. Died September 1, 1912', *The Musical Times*, 53/836 (1 Oct. 1912), 638.

4   'Mr. S. Coleridge-Taylor's "Hiawatha"', *The Musical Times and Singing Class Circular*, 41/686 (1 Apr. 1900), 246.

5   *The Daily Mail*, 23 March 1900.

6   See Frank Howes, *The English Musical Renaissance* (London: Secker and Warburg, 1966), where Coleridge-Taylor is mentioned only once, obliquely, and Peter J. Pirie, *The English Musical Renaissance* (London: Gollancz, 1979), in which he is entirely absent. The composer is also not to be found in Ernest Walker, *A History of Music in England* (London: Oxford University Press/H. Milford, 1907), published in his lifetime, though later editions from 1924 and 1952 devote a single paragraph to him.

7   The idea stems from the critic J. A. Fuller-Maitland and was developed by Walker, *A History of Music in England*, and Howes, *The English Musical Renaissance*.

8   See Benedict Taylor, *Arthur Sullivan: A Musical Reappraisal (Music in Nineteenth-Century Britain)* (Abingdon: Routledge, 2017), p. 8. The phrase in fact repeats Byron's account of his early success with *Childe Harold*.

9   There are occasional accounts of contemporaries not being able to place Coleridge-Taylor's ethnic background: Sayers tells of a passenger on a train who decided that the composer was most likely Japanese from his appearance (*Samuel Coleridge-Taylor*, pp. 257–8).

10 The original campaign was initiated by Patrick Vernon in response to an earlier '100 Greatest Britons' BBC poll; see https://www.100greatblackbritons.co.uk.

11 'Visit of English Negro Composer Emphasizes American Prejudice', *New York Times*, 27 Nov. 1904.

12 Booker T. Washington, Preface to *Twenty-Four Negro Melodies. Transcribed for the Piano by S. Coleridge-Taylor, Op. 59* (Boston: Ditson, n.d. [1905]), p. ix. J. Hillary Taylor, 'Chats on Music and Music Study. 8: S. Coleridge Taylor', *The Washington Bee*, 18 Mar. 1911, p. 6.

13 Douglas Lorimer, *Science, Race Relations and Resistance: Britain, 1870–1914 (Studies in Imperialism)* (Manchester: Manchester University Press, 2013), p. 5; 'Reconstructing Victorian Racial Discourse: Images of Race, the Language of Race Relations, and the Context of Black Resistance', in Gretchen Holbrook Gerzina (ed.), *Black Victorians, Black Victoriana* (New Brunswick, NJ: Rutgers University Press, 2003), p. 187.

14 An accessible introduction to some of these issues is given by William Weber, 'The History of Musical Canon', in Nicholas Cook and Mark Everist (eds.), *Rethinking Music* (New York: Oxford University Press, 1999), pp. 336–55.

CHAPTER 2

1 'Mr. S. Coleridge Taylor's Concert', *The Musical Times and Singing Class Circular*, 38/653 (1 July 1897), 465.

2 *The Musical Times* was owned by the publishers Novello, who would be closely associated with Coleridge-Taylor through the success of the *Hiawatha* cantatas; but both pieces named were in fact published by the rival firm of Augener, so there is little sense this review could be simply a sales pitch.

3 As related by his half-sister, Marjorie Evans: 'I Remember Coleridge: Recollections of Samuel Coleridge-Taylor (1875-1912)', in Rainer Lotz and Ian Pegg (eds.), *Under the Imperial Carpet: Essays in Black History 1780-1950* (Crawley: Rabbit Press, 1986), p. 34.

4 On the indeterminate evidence for contact between father and son, see Jeffrey Green, *Samuel Coleridge-Taylor, a Musical Life* (London: Pickering and Chatto, 2011), p. 91.

5 For a detailed account of this background, see Jeffrey Green, 'Samuel Coleridge-Taylor: The Early Years', *Black Music Research Journal*, 21 (2001), 133–57. The composer himself seems to have been reticent to give too much detail on his family background in published interviews but did hold that his parents had been married (which might have been a sincere belief).

6 Though claimed as married in the 1891 census return, no marriage registration has been found for the two; see ibid., 146.

7 The interview is printed as 'Mr. Coleridge-Taylor', *The Musical Times*, 50/793 (1 Mar. 1909), 153.

8 Ibid., 153–4.

9 Ibid., 153.

10 See the story related by Sayers, *Samuel Coleridge-Taylor*, pp. 26–7.

11 *Norwood News* (9 June 1906), 8.

12 'The Late S. Coleridge-Taylor', *The Musical Herald* (1 Oct. 1912), 296–7.

13 See Sayers, *Samuel Coleridge-Taylor*, pp. 84–5, 240; Havergal Brian [La main gauche], 'On the other hand', *Musical Opinion* (Sept. 1934), 1023.

14 Jeremy Dibble, *Charles Villiers Stanford: Man and Musician* (Oxford: Clarendon Press, 2002), p. 270.

15 Letter from Jaeger to Elgar, 15 September 1897 (*GB-EBm L9175*), quoted in Catherine Carr, *The Music of Samuel Coleridge-Taylor (1875–1912): A Critical and Analytical Study*, PhD diss., Durham University, 2005, p. 104.

16 Elgar, letter to Herbert Brewer, quoted in A. H. Brewer, *Memories of Choirs and Cloisters (Fifty Years of Music)* (London: John Lane, 1931), p. 93.

17 Jaeger to Brewer, 12 May 1898, quoted in ibid., p. 94.

18 'Gloucester Musical Festival', *The Musical Times and Singing Class Circular*, 39/668 (1 Oct. 1898), 667.

19 The assumption is made clearly in a posthumous survey from 1920: 'doubtless largely due to the strong atavistic strain in his nature . . . his subconscious self retained the instincts of his primitive paternal race and translated their spirit into music.' George Lowe, 'The Choral Works of S. Coleridge-Taylor', *The Musical Times*, 61/931 (1 Sept. 1920), 598. But it is widespread in criticism from the first decades of the century.

20 'Mr. S. Coleridge Taylor's Concert'. An even earlier review exhibits this same association ('because the composer is partly of African descent the remarkable use made of various rhythmic devices and the prominence of the barbaric element thus acquire peculiar significance.' 'Ballade in D Minor. For Violin and Pianoforte by S. Coleridge-Taylor', *The Musical Times and Singing Class Circular*, 36/630 (1 Aug. 1895), 532).

21 Reviews in *The Standard*, *Daily Graphic*, and *Times*, reproduced in *The Musical Times* (1 Oct. 1898), 695.

22 Herbert Antcliffe, 'Some Notes on Coleridge-Taylor', *The Musical Quarterly*, 8/2 (1922), 182. Antcliffe's account is nevertheless filled with dubious racial theorizing.

23 Reporting on *Hiawatha*: 'a few years ago, [Taylor] sometimes produced works which, in their untrammelled boisterousness, not to say wildness, savoured of that "barbarity" which we find in the worst—i.e., most intensely "national"—Russian music' ('Hiawatha's Wedding-Feast. A Cantata for Tenor Solo, Chorus, and Orchestra by S. Coleridge-Taylor', *The Musical Times and Singing Class Circular*, 39/668 (1 Oct. 1898), 673). 'Like Tschaïkowsky in

his most characteristic movements, there is a certain barbaric opulence about his music' ('Mr. Coleridge-Taylor's "Hiawatha's Wedding Feast" at Sunderland', *The Musical Times and Singing Class Circular*, 39/670 (1 Dec. 1898), 815).

24 'Mr. S. Coleridge-Taylor's "Hiawatha"', *The Musical Times*, 41/686 (1 Apr. 1900), 246.

25 Jaeger, letter to Elgar, 15 Sept. 1897, quoted in Carr, *The Music of Samuel Coleridge-Taylor*, p. 104. Jaeger uses a term to describe Daniel Taylor's racial background that is now taboo, but in his historical and cultural context may well not have been intended to be disparaging.

26 Jaeger, letter to Brewer, 12 May 1898, quoted in Brewer, *Memories of Choirs and Cloisters*, p. 94.

27 A notorious example of this association is Hubert Parry's memorial. See 'Samuel Coleridge-Taylor. Born August 15, 1875. Died September 1, 1912', *The Musical Times*, 53/836 (1 Oct. 1912), 638.

28 'Mr. Coleridge-Taylor', 156.

29 Throughout the following discussion I use the term 'exotic' to denote the depiction of a different people, their culture, locale, and elements associated with it, primarily 'as others', for the appeal of their alterity from the observers' own standpoint. The depiction may obviously have little relation to the group's self-representation, and in many cases can appear essentialized, racialized, or otherwise problematic from our own current standpoint. For more detailed discussion of the idea in nineteenth-century music, see especially Ralph P. Locke, *Musical Exoticism: Images and Reflections* (Cambridge: Cambridge University Press, 2009).

30 Miriam W. Barndt-Webb, 'Longfellow, Henry Wadsworth', in Stanley Sadie (ed.), *The New Grove Dictionary of Music and Musicians*, 2nd edition, 29 vols. (London: Macmillan, 2001), vol. XV, p. 168.

31 The links are divulged in an interview quoted in the *New York Herald*, 15 Dec. 1893; see Michael Beckerman, *New Worlds of Dvořák* (New York: Norton, 2003), pp. 25–6, and on the operatic plans, 66–76.

CHAPTER 3

1 Letter from Elgar to Jaeger, undated, June or early July 1898. Percy M. Young (ed.), *Letters to Nimrod: Edward Elgar to August Jaeger, 1897–1908* (London: Dennis Dobson, 1965), p. 14.

2 Letter from Jaeger to Elgar, 1 Nov. 1899. *Gb-EBm L8385*, quoted in Carr, *The Music of Samuel Coleridge-Taylor*, p. 108.

3 'Mr. S. Coleridge-Taylor's "Hiawatha"', *The Musical Times*, 41/686 (1 Apr. 1900), 246.

4 Ibid.
5 Mrs J. F. Coleridge-Taylor, *Genius and Musician: A Memory Sketch or Personal Reminiscences of my Husband. Genius and Musician S. Coleridge-Taylor 1875–1912* (Bognor Regis and London: John Crowther Ltd., n.d. [*c.*1943]), p. 11.
6 *New York Herald*, 15 Dec. 1893.
7 See Michael Beckerman, *New Worlds of Dvořák* (New York: Norton, 2003), pp. 25–6.
8 'Hiawatha's Wedding-Feast. A Cantata for Tenor Solo, Chorus, and Orchestra by S. Coleridge-Taylor' [score], *The Musical Times and Singing Class Circular*, 39/668 (1 Oct. 1898), 673.
9 A. Kaufmann, 'Hiawatha a Classic: Great Work of the Famous Negro Composer', *The Washington Post*, 10 Apr. 1904, p. 8.
10 'Hiawatha's Wedding-Feast', 673.
11 An African American critic remarked in this context on how 'Mr Taylor has given some "semblance" of the weird repetition music of those [Native American] people. . . . [H]e tells of them in those monotonous tones and chantlike, that stiff Indian dignity and reserve'. W. Milton Lewis, 'Pencilings', *The Freeman*, 6 Aug. 1904, p. 4.
12 These themes include the opening soprano number 'Spring had come', the tenor's following 'He had seen', and 'Only Hiawatha' (rehearsal 18), and those at rehearsals 40 and 51/52.
13 *Hiawatha* was not alone in this: Sullivan's 1880 *The Martyr of Antioch*, billed as a 'sacred musical drama', was staged by the Carl Rosa Opera company in 1898. On the various narrative and dramatic modes used in British choral works of the late nineteenth century, see Charles Edward McGuire, *Elgar's Oratorios: The Creation of an Epic Narrative* (Aldershot: Ashgate, 2002), esp. ch. 2.
14 The role of these linking passages is clearly evident though their excision in the 1930s Malcolm Sargent / Royal Choral Society recordings, especially in *The Death of Minnehaha* (1931), which cuts several minutes of material between the choral passages.
15 A. J. Jaeger, 'Analytical Notes' for Royal Choral Society concert, *Scenes from the Song of Hiawatha* (London: Novello, 1903), 23, quoted in Carr, *The Music of Samuel Coleridge-Taylor*, p. 117.
16 Rendered as 'Spring had come with all its splendour' by the composer.
17 As explained at the end of this chapter, there is a salient reminder of the trilogy's opening motive at this point; perhaps it is the thematic signal here that inspired Jaeger's interpretation, overriding other formal, tonal, and narrative considerations. Beyond earlier hybrid works like Beethoven's Ninth Symphony and Mendelssohn's *Lobgesang* there was, in fact, precedent in Britain for merging a choral work with the design of an orchestral symphony. Elgar's own earlier Longfellow cantata, *The Black Knight* (1891), was

described by the composer as a symphony for chorus and orchestra, though it is much easier to read the first scene as a sonata-form movement and rather less a stretch to conceive the four parts as akin in their smaller size and character to symphonic movements.

CHAPTER 4

1 No less questionable, and distinctly more gratuitous, is the suggestion of antisemitism in this final canto, as the priestly 'Black-Robe chief, the prophet' of the Pale-faced arrivals spreads the Gospel to the Native Americans. He tells of Mary, of Jesus, and of 'the Jews, the tribe accursed', who 'Mocked him, scourged him, crucified him'. Such expressions, while regrettable, are not uncommon in the two-thousand-year history of Christianity, but their introduction seems out of place in a purported Native American epic. These lines were also set by Coleridge-Taylor.

2 Brad Fruhauff, 'The Lost Work of Longfellow's *Hiawatha*', *The Journal of the Midwest Modern Language Association*, 40/2 (2007), 79–96 at 79.

3 Dana Gioia, 'Longfellow in the Aftermath of Modernism', in Jay Parini (ed.), *The Columbia History of American Poetry* (New York: Columbia University Press, 1993), pp. 64–96 at 64, 65.

4 Daniel Aaron, 'Introduction' to Henry Wadsworth Longfellow, *The Song of Hiawatha* (London: Dent/Everyman, 2004), pp. xi–xix at xiv.

5 For example, Alan Trachtenberg, *Shades of Hiawatha: Staging Indians, Making Americans, 1880–1930* (New York: Hill and Wang, 2004). On the poem's global reach, see Katie Flint, ' "Is the Native an American?": National Identity and the British Reception of *Hiawatha*', and Tavia Nyong'o, '*Hiawatha*'s Black Atlantic Itineraries', in Meredith L. McGill (ed.), *The Traffic in Poems: Nineteenth-Century Poetry and Transatlantic Exchange* (New Brunswick: Rutgers University Press, 2008), pp. 63–80 and 81–96.

6 Alan Trachtenberg, 'Singing Hiawatha: Longfellow's Hybrid Myth of America', *Yale Review*, 90/1 (2002), 4.

7 On parodies of *Hiawatha*, see William Logan, 'Longfellow's *Hiawatha*, Carroll's *Hiawatha*: The Name and Nature of Parody', *The Hopkins Review*, 5/4 (2012), 534–62. 'Some poems are self-parodic before they're ever parodied' Logan comments laconically (552).

8 Longfellow, letter to T. C. Callicot, 29 Nov. 1855, quoted in Ernest J. Moyne and Tuano F. Mustanoja, 'Longfellow's *Song of Hiawatha* and *Kalevala*', *American Literature*, 25/1 (1953), 87–9 at 89.

9 Aaron, 'Introduction', p. xii.

10 Fruhauff, 'The Lost Work of Longfellow's *Hiawatha*', 81.

11 Ibid., 81. Fruhauff sees Longfellow's pastoral as poised between idyll (the first half, culminating in the invention of picture writing in canto 14) and elegy (the troubles that emerge over the second part).

12 Ibid., 82.

13 Patrick Brantlinger, *Dark Vanishings: Discourse on the Extinction of Primitive Races, 1800–1930* (Ithaca: Cornell University Press, 2003), p. 3. See further John Hay, 'Narratives of Extinction and the Last Man', in *Postapocalyptic Fantasies in Antebellum American Literature* (Cambridge: Cambridge University Press, 2017), p. 90.

14 Henry Wadsworth Longfellow, 'The Literary Spirit of Our Country' (1824), in *Poems and Other Writings* (New York: Library of America, 2000), p. 794.

15 Fruhauff, 'The Lost Work of Longfellow's *Hiawatha*', 91–2.

16 Ibid., 93.

17 'The Prologue claims that the stories come from the land and people together—or from the land that produced a people, even from the land identified with a people'. Ibid., 84.

18 W. C. Berwick Sayers, *Samuel Coleridge-Taylor, Musician: His Life and Letters* (London: Cassell, 1915, rev. ed. Augener, 1927), p. 57; 'Mr. Coleridge-Taylor', *The Musical Times*, 50/793 (1 Mar. 1909), 156.

19 Michael V. Pisani, *Imagining Native America in Music* (New Haven: Yale University Press, 2005), p. 157.

20 An attempt along these lines, and possible illustration of its dangers, is given in Nicholas Cook, 'The Imaginary African: Race, Identity, and Samuel Coleridge-Taylor', in Raymond MacDonald, David J. Hargreaves, and Dorothy Miell (eds.), *Handbook of Musical Identities* (New York: Oxford University Press, 2017), pp. 710–12.

21 The progression from D minor to F major is conventional enough, but the tortuous way in which it is achieved—via a diminished seventh—sounds far more unsettling. It recalls in fact the opening of Coleridge-Taylor's Ballade in A minor.

22 Meirion Hughes and Robert Stradling, *The English Musical Renaissance 1840–1940: Constructing a National Music*, originally pub. 1993, revised 2nd edition (Manchester: Manchester University Press, 2001), p. 249.

CHAPTER 5

1 Despite the common opus number, its status as a 'distinct work' was emphasized on publication, which perhaps didn't help. Choral societies without recourse to an orchestra would have inevitably omitted it.

2 The music and text should not be confused with the similarly titled and better-known spiritual 'Nobody knows the trouble I've seen'.

3 See Ellsworth Janifer, 'Samuel Coleridge-Taylor in Washington', *Phylon*, 28/2 (1967), 187–8.

4 Doris Evans McGinty, ' "That You Came so Far to See Us": Coleridge-Taylor in America', *Black Music Research Journal*, 21/2 (2001), 199.

5 *The Freeman*, 17 Feb. 1900, p. 5.

6 'Musical Idol of London', *Afro-American*, 6 June 1903, p. 1 (a few typos tacitly corrected).

7 Janifer, 'Samuel Coleridge-Taylor in Washington', 195.

8 See Doris Evans McGinty, 'Black Women in the Music of Washington, D.C., 1900–20', in Josephine Wright with Samuel Floyd, Jr. (eds.), *New Perspectives on Music: Essays in Honor of Eileen Southern* (Warren, MI: Harmonie Park Press, 1992), pp. 409–49.

9 Programme, S. Coleridge-Taylor Choral Society, S. Coleridge-Taylor's *Hiawatha*, 16, 17, & 18 November 1904, p. 13. Available at https://www.loc.gov/item/91898526/.

10 Mamie Hilyer's tribute, written following the composer's death in 1912, is contained in Sayers, *Samuel Coleridge-Taylor*, pp. 108–9.

11 *The Washington Bee*, 29 Mar. 1902, p. 8.

12 'A Negro's music as sung by a chorus of Negroes', *New York Times*, 3 May 1903, p. 2.

13 'Occasional Notes', *The Musical Times and Singing Class Circular*, 44/727 (1 Sept. 1903), 591.

14 A. Kaufmann, 'Hiawatha a Classic: Great Work of the Famous Negro Composer', *The Washington Post*, 10 Apr. 1904, p. 8.

15 'The United States Marine band orchestra was hardly up to what might have been expected of it, several times spoiling the delicate passages that exist in the work.' In contrast, 'the chorus, outside of the composer, was the feature of the evening, and showed by its marvelous performance the long and careful training which it has undergone', though interestingly the paper reports that 'the soloists were, to some extent, somewhat faulty'. 'Hiawatha at the Lyric', *Afro-American*, 26 Nov. 1904, p. 4.

16 'Under Composer's Baton: "Hiawatha" Rendered by the Coleridge-Taylor Choral Society', *The Washington Post*, 17 Nov. 1904, p. 9

17 Kaufmann, 'Hiawatha a Classic'.

18 'Visit of English Negro Composer Emphasizes American Prejudice', *New York Times*, 27 Nov. 1904.

19 'Musical Idol of London', drawing on the *New York Times*'s 'A Negro's music as sung by a chorus of Negroes'. A report of an incident of racial abuse suffered by the composer on his first visit to the US ('A Common White Man. Attempts To Insult S. Coleridge-Taylor, On A Railroad Train Between This City And Washington', *Afro-American*, 26 Nov. 1904, p. 5) was taken entirely from the (white) *Baltimore Sunday Herald*.

20 On the (arguably largely ineffective) attempts by Black communities to gain respect and admittance through achievements in (white) classical musical culture see Lawrence Schenbeck, *Racial Uplift and American Music, 1878–1943* (Jackson, MS: University Press of Mississippi, 2012), esp. ch. 2.

21 'Flawless Production of "Hiawatha"', *Washington Bee*, 2 May 1908, p. 5; 'Colored Skin Made Lighter By Use of Wonderine'. Such adverts—for products to make skin paler or to straighten 'knotty' hair—are far from uncommon in this period in the *Bee*.

22 Anna J. Cooper, 'Reminiscences' (*Manuscripts for the Grimke Book*, 33, typescript, p. 3), http://dh.howard.edu/ajc_grimke_ manuscripts/33 (accessed 14 Sept. 2022).

23 E. Azalia Hackley, 'The Musical Progress of the Race during the Last Year', *The Freeman*, 18 Dec. 1915, p. 20.

24 As Alan Trachtenberg shows in *Shades of Hiawatha*, the white reception of Longfellow's poem around the turn of the twentieth century reveals how *Hiawatha* was remobilized to understand 'race-relations' and construct a sense of Euroamerican identity vis-à-vis African Americans.

25 As reported by W. C. Berwick Sayers (*Samuel Coleridge-Taylor, Musician: His Life and Letters* (London: Cassell, 1915, rev. ed. Augener, 1927), p. 149); in a reply to Hilyer he similarly pronounced it 'about the finest book I have ever read by a coloured man and one of the best by any author, white or black'. Letter to A. F. Hilyer, 14 Sept. 1904, in ibid.

26 W. E. B. Du Bois, *The Souls of Black Folk: Essays and Sketches* (Chicago: A. C. McClurg & Co., 1903), p. 251.

27 McGinty, '"That You Came so Far to See Us"', 202.

28 *Jubilee Songs: As Sung by the Jubilee Singers*, edited by Theodore F. Seward and George L. White (New York: Biglow & Main, 1872), p. 9.

29 There is some uncertainty in commentaries whether the overture is meant to precede the three cantatas or form an entr'acte between the second and third parts (see, for instance, William Tortolano, *Samuel Coleridge-Taylor: Anglo-Black composer, 1875– 1912*, 2nd edition (Lanham, MD: Scarecrow Press, 2002), p. 20). The latter view seems to be the result of the numbering within the opus (the overture as the third of the four pieces, following compositional genesis), but otherwise has little to recommend it: musically there are stronger reasons for placing it first (for the reasons given above), and it is unusual not to play an overture at the start. Accounts from Coleridge-Taylor's lifetime imply that an opening position was assumed.

30 Booker T. Washington, Preface to *Twenty-Four Negro Melodies. Transcribed for the Piano by S. Coleridge-Taylor, Op. 59* (Boston: Ditson, n.d. [1905]), p. ix. Du Bois, we remember, had gone further in asserting that only the 'Negro folk-song' stood as American music.

31 McGinty, '"That You Came so Far to See Us"', 209.

32 W. Milton Lewis, 'Pencilings. J. [sic] Coleridge-Taylor—Hiawatha', The Freeman, 6 Aug. 1904, p. 4, punctuation slightly amended. See also George Revill, 'Hiawatha and Pan-Africanism: Samuel Coleridge-Taylor (1875–1912), a black composer in suburban London', Ecumene, 2/3 (1995), 253.

33 Du Bois, The Souls of Black Folk, p. 253.

34 Published in 'The Late S. Coleridge-Taylor', The Musical Herald (1 Oct. 1912), 297.

35 Havergal Brian [La main gauche], 'On the other hand', Musical Opinion (Sept. 1934), 1023.

36 See Geoffrey Self, The Hiawatha Man: The Life and Work of Samuel Coleridge-Taylor (Aldershot: Scolar Press, 1995), p. vii.

37 Sayers, S. Coleridge-Taylor, p. 90.

38 Self, The Hiawatha Man, p. 91.

39 Paul Richards, 'A Pan-African Composer? Coleridge-Taylor and Africa', Black Music Research Journal, 21 (2001), 248, 239

40 Most notable is probably his public declaration that 'personally, I consider myself the equal of any white man who ever lived'; Coleridge-Taylor, letter to the editor of Croydon Guardian, February 1912, quoted in Sayers, S. Coleridge-Taylor, p. 271 (the entire letter is reproduced pp. 270–2).

41 There are some works that suggest sympathy with decolonizing activities on the part of Black figures, but none to my knowledge that manifest clear reproof of US settler colonialism or the existence of Britain's contemporary empire. At the age of twenty-one, Coleridge-Taylor published a poem in the African Times celebrating the fiftieth anniversary of Liberian independence (see Jeffrey Green, Samuel Coleridge-Taylor, a Musical Life (London: Pickering and Chatto, 2011), p. 89). Liberia, Sierra Leone's southern neighbour, had declared independence from the United States in 1847, making it the first modern African republic. But while the US had refused to recognize the new state for some decades, Britain had done so immediately, so the gesture was hardly provocative fifty years later in England. His 1901 orchestral work Toussaint l'Ouverture commemorates the eponymous Black military hero, instrumental in the Haitian Revolution, but again this need not imply anything more than a possible interest in a prominent Black historical figure.

42 Marc Matera, Black London: The Imperial Metropolis and Decolonization in the Twentieth Century (Berkeley: University of California Press, 2015); writing of Black British identity in the early twentieth century, Matera remarks 'Africans and Afro-Caribbeans thought and acted as participants in two different extranational "affective communities": as aspirational imperial citizens within the juridical and political space of the British imperium, and as members of a transimperial collectivity of people of African descent' (p. 5).

43 Jonathan Schneer, 'Anti-Imperial London: The Pan-African Conference of 1900', in Gretchen Holbrook Gerzina (ed.), *Black Victorians, Black Victoriana* (New Brunswick, NJ: Rutgers University Press, 2003), p. 175.

44 Self, *The Hiawatha Man*, p. 143. As Self observes, the question of whether Coleridge-Taylor was a Black Englishman or 'an African living in a foreign country' is 'a difficult question to approach, since it is in the field of perception: how he perceived himself and how others perceived him. And the "others" themselves would have a varying perception according to whether they were in the United States or in the United Kingdom. In any case, many people have no settled "persona". It may vary with circumstances or with whom the subject may be interacting.' For a slightly different perspective, see Nicholas Cook, 'The Imaginary African: Race, Identity, and Samuel Coleridge-Taylor', in Raymond MacDonald, David J. Hargreaves, and Dorothy Miell (eds.), *Handbook of Musical Identities* (New York: Oxford University Press, 2017), pp. 703–21.

45 J. F. Coleridge-Taylor, *Genius and Musician: A Memory Sketch*, p. 59. The wording in an earlier account she gave to Sayers is reported slightly differently: 'When I die the papers will call me a creole'; Sayers, *S. Coleridge-Taylor*, p. 306.

46 'The composer was probably fretting about [critics] drawing attention to his mixed racial origins, in an era when language and culture were thought about in evolutionary terms.' Richards, 'A Pan-African Composer?', 255.

47 Tortolano, *Samuel Coleridge-Taylor*, p. 3.

48 Sidney Butterworth, 'Coleridge-Taylor: New Facts and Old Fiction', *Musical Times*, 130/1754 (Apr. 1989), 203.

49 Sayers, *Samuel Coleridge-Taylor*, p. 252: 'He hated the early criticisms which dealt equally with his skin and his music'; he claimed 'he was a British musician with an English education, and that he desired to be estimated in his relation to music and not to the music of the negro only'. Again, however, Sayers is writing from a particular (white English) perspective, and indeed perpetrates some of the same questionable assumptions he appears to decry.

50 Richards, 'A Pan-African Composer?', 256.

51 Akin Euba, review of *Samuel Coleridge-Taylor: The Development of His Compositional Style* by Jewel Taylor Thompson, *Research in African Literatures*, 32/2, 'The Landscape of African Music' (2001), 207.

CHAPTER 6

1 W. C. Berwick Sayers, *Samuel Coleridge-Taylor, Musician: His Life and Letters* (London: Cassell, 1915, rev. ed. Augener, 1927), p. 290. The composer's daughter later claimed that Fletcher misrepresented her father's

conception; see Avril Coleridge-Taylor, *The Heritage of Samuel Coleridge-Taylor* (London: Dennis Dobson, 1979), pp. 78–81.

2 Jeffrey Green, *Samuel Coleridge-Taylor, a Musical Life* (London: Pickering and Chatto, 2011), pp. 185–6. For a brief summary of the interwar stagings see also his 'Requiem: "Hiawatha" in the 1920s and 1930s', *Black Music Research Journal*, 21/2 (2001), 283–8.

3 Sargent took over for the 1925 season, and was absent only in 1933 and 1934 owing to serious illness; Geoffrey Toye and Albert Coates stood in for these two seasons. Sargent would continue conducting concert performances of *Hiawatha* with the Royal Choral Society into the 1960s and making a fine recording of the first cantata with them in 1962.

4 *Hiawatha's Wedding Feast*, Walter Glynne, Royal Choral Society, Orchestra, Malcolm Sargent, HMV, 1930; *The Death of Minnehaha*, Elsie Suddaby, Howard Fry, George Baker, Royal Choral Society, Orchestra, Malcolm Sargent, HMV, 1931

5 Arrangement by H. A. Chambers, advertised in *The Musical Times*, 75/1099 (Sept. 1934), 849. The absence of the composer's name on the cover is striking.

6 The 'London Coronation Choir' and London Symphony Orchestra, conducted by Colin Ratcliffe, producer Powell Lloyd, held in the Royal Albert Hall from 29 June to 11 July 1953. Euphan Maclaren, the choreographer since 1925, was the primary link with the pre-war productions.

7 Nicholas Cook, 'The Imaginary African: Race, Identity, and Samuel Coleridge-Taylor', in Raymond MacDonald, David J. Hargreaves, and Dorothy Miell (eds.), *Handbook of Musical Identities* (New York: Oxford University Press, 2017), p. 719. To this extent an analogy might be drawn with the popularity of blackface minstrelsy in earlier times.

8 The synopsis is included in the 1925 programme and used thereafter in following years.

9 'Music in the Provinces', *The Musical Times*, 51/814 (1 Dec. 1910), 804. See also Green, *Samuel Coleridge-Taylor*, p. 185.

10 Doris Evans McGinty, ' "That You Came so Far to See Us": Coleridge-Taylor in America', *Black Music Research Journal*, 21/2 (2001), 197–234.

11 *Howard University Record*, 1/2 (1907), 13; *The Echo* (Yearbook of Howard University) 1920, n.p.

12 ' "Hiawatha" was an Artistic Success', *Afro-American*, 8 May 1926, p. 6; 'Choral Society to Sing "Hiawatha" ', *Afro-American*, 21 May 1927, p. 8; 'Official Program Natl. Asso. Colored Women's Clubs', *Afro-American*, 4 Aug. 1928, p. 3. Wilson was later fondly recalled by students as having giving 'loving instruction in singing the beautiful Hiawatha choral trilogy.' ('Betty Moss, 'If You As Me', *Afro-American*, 1 Jan. 1972, p. 5).

13 McGinty, ' "That You Came so Far to See Us" ', 230.

14 As this demonstrates, there were other musical groups besides the Washington choral society who named themselves after the composer. Another example would be the 'S. Coleridge-Taylor orchestra' operating at Wilberforce University in the early years of the century.

15 For instance, *Hiawatha* still featured at a National Association of Negro Musicians meeting at Delaware State College, 1960 (*Afro-American*, 27 Aug. 1960).

16 Earl Calloway, 'The Artists' Circle', *Afro-American*, 10 Dec. 1966, p. 11.

17 The solo from *Hiawatha* was coupled with the 'Danse Nègre' from the *African Suite*, Op. 35, and William Grant Still's *Afro-American* Symphony; LSO/Paul Freeman, with tenor William Brown, Columbia Masterworks M 32782 (1974).

18 See for instance Samantha Ege, 'Nora Douglas Holt's Teachings of a Black Classical Canon', in J. Daniel Jenkins (ed.), *The Oxford Handbook of Public Music Theory* (2022; online edition, Oxford Academic, 13 Oct. 2021), https://doi.org/ 10.1093/oxfordhb/9780197551554.013.21, accessed 28 Sept. 2023.

19 Frank Wesley Clelland, 'Samuel Coleridge-Taylor, Musician', in Philip Henry Lotz (ed.), *Rising Above Color (Creative Personalities Volume V)* (New York: Association Press, 1946), pp. 38–49.

20 Philip Henry Lotz, 'Introduction', *Rising Above Color*, p. vii.

21 Clelland, 'Samuel Coleridge-Taylor, Musician', p. 48.

22 Ellsworth Janifer, 'Samuel Coleridge-Taylor in Washington', *Phylon*, 28/2 (1967), 193 (echoing Sayers, *Samuel Coleridge-Taylor*, p. 162). The comment is nevertheless a striking non sequitur, following on as it does directly from Janifer's account of the *New York Times* interview of 27 Nov. 1904: 'He is stiffly, calmly English in every inch, so English that a blind man would be moved to jeers that there was a drop of other blood in him.'

23 'Doings of Stage Folks', *Washington Colored American* (1900), 6; quoted in McGinty, ' "That You Came so Far to See Us" ', 200. Inside the article Coleridge-Taylor is described more accurately as 'a man of African blood'— yet one who was merely 'resident in England'.

24 Dan Godfrey, *Memories and Music* (London: Hutchinson & Co., 1924), p. 97.

25 <https://en.wikipedia.org/wiki/Samuel_Coleridge-Taylor>, last accessed 22 Feb. 2024. The passage concludes: 'At one stage Coleridge-Taylor seriously considered emigrating to the United States, as he was intrigued by his father's family's past there.' The alleged interest in his supposed American ancestry seems a colourful embellishment to a suggestion about his 'contemplating the desirability of emigrating' made briefly by Sayers (*Samuel Coleridge-Taylor*, p. 170). If Coleridge-Taylor had thought he had been descended from African Americans it would be remarkable that he did not mention this in his interviews with US newspapers or to the many African Americans who befriended him; instead, he simply points to his father's origins in Africa.

26 Paul Richards, 'A Pan-African Composer? Coleridge-Taylor and Africa', *Black Music Research Journal*, 21 (2001), 244–5; Jeffrey Green, 'Samuel Coleridge-Taylor: The Early Years', *Black Music Research Journal*, 21 (2001), 133–4.

27 Frank Howes, *The English Musical Renaissance* (1966), where Coleridge-Taylor is named once, obliquely, and Peter Pirie, *The English Musical Renaissance* (1979), in which he is not mentioned at all.

28 31 Oct. 1974, from Fairfield Halls, Croydon; the BBC Singers and Concert Orchestra, conducted by Kenneth Alwyn.

29 Andrew Clements, review of *The Song of Hiawatha*, *The Guardian*, 5 Aug. 2013, https://www.theguardian.com/music/2013/aug/05/the-song-of-hiawatha-gloucester-review.

30 Sayers relates the composer was sceptical towards this idea ('Devotion to light music, he thought, destroyed one's higher inspiration'), though notes he modified this view in his last years (*Samuel Coleridge-Taylor*, p. 96).

31 'Hiawatha's Wedding-Feast', *Musical Times* (1 Oct. 1898), 674. Likewise, in the December issue, 'Here we do not of course, consider the little cantata a great masterpiece . . . He will do much better yet, for he has the gifts and strength and the modesty for higher things'. 'The Royal College of Music', *The Musical Times and Singing Class Circular*, 39/670 (1 Dec. 1898), 808.

32 Reported in *The Times*, 23 May 1902.

33 See also Meirion Hughes and Robert Stradling, *The English Musical Renaissance 1840–1940: Constructing a National Music*, originally pub. 1993, revised 2nd edition (Manchester: Manchester University Press, 2001), p. 247. Beyond the example of Edward German, mentioned above, Arthur Sullivan offers an instructive parallel case. His 1886 Longfellow cantata, *The Golden Legend*, was the one British choral work to rival *Hiawatha* in popularity before the First World War, but fell from favour rapidly thereafter, along with virtually all of his music bar the comic operas with Gilbert.

34 Akin Euba, review of *Samuel Coleridge-Taylor: The Development of His Compositional Style* by Jewel Taylor Thompson, *Research in African Literatures*, 32/2, 'The Landscape of African Music' (2001), 207.

FURTHER READING AND RESOURCES

READING

Basic Biographical Works

Coleridge-Taylor, Avril: *The Heritage of Samuel Coleridge-Taylor* (London: Dennis Dobson, 1979). A short account by the composer's daughter.

Coleridge-Taylor, Jessie: *A Memory Sketch or Personal Reminiscences of My Husband. Genius and Musician—S. Coleridge-Taylor 1875–1912* (Bognor Regis: John Crowther, Ltd., n.d. [1943]). A short account by the composer's widow.

Green, Jeffrey: *Samuel Coleridge-Taylor, A Music Life* (London: Pickering & Chatto, 2011). The most accurate and detailed modern account of Coleridge-Taylor's life, providing an important correction to some of the inaccuracies perpetuated in many earlier narratives.

Sayers, W. C. Berwick: *Samuel Coleridge-Taylor, Musician: His Life and Letters* (London: Cassell, 1915, rev. ed. Augener, 1927). The first full biography, written posthumously by a friend of the composer. Some inaccuracies and fabrications, but nevertheless the primary port of call.

More Specialized Studies

Black Music Research Journal, Special Issue: Samuel Coleridge-Taylor, ed. Jeffrey Green, 21/2 (2011), 217–302. Contains a multitude of useful articles by Dominique-René de Lerma, Jeffrey Green, Charles Kay, Catherine Carr, Doris Evans McGinty, Paul Richards, and Geoffrey Self.

Carr, Catherine: *The Music of Samuel Coleridge-Taylor (1875–1912): A Critical and Analytical Study*. PhD diss., Durham University, 2005.

Cook, Nicholas: 'The Imaginary African: Race, Identity, and Samuel Coleridge-Taylor', in Raymond MacDonald, David J. Hargreaves, and Dorothy Miell (eds.), *Handbook of Musical Identities* (New York: Oxford University Press, 2017), pp. 703–21.

CONTEXTUAL WORKS

Historical Sources

Du Bois, W. E. B.: *The Souls of Black Folk: Essays and Sketches* (Chicago: A. C. McClurg & Co., 1903). An eloquent, passionate, and often poetic account by a leading Black intellectual and activist, described by Coleridge-Taylor as one of the finest books he had ever read.

Washington, Booker T.: Preface to *Twenty-Four Negro Melodies*, by Samuel Coleridge-Taylor (Boston: Ditson, 1905). A tribute to Coleridge-Taylor by one of the most prominent African American intellectuals and educators.

Wells, H. G.: 'The Tragedy of Colour', in *The Future in America: A Search After Realities* (London: Chapman and Hall, 1906), pp. 257–81. A sympathetic account by a leading white English author of the contemporary difficulties faced by African Americans, influenced by Booker T. Washington. Coleridge-Taylor recommended this chapter to his British contemporaries.

History/Theory

Gilroy, Paul: *The Black Atlantic: Modernity and Double Consciousness* (Cambridge, MA: Harvard University Press, 1993).

Green, Jeffrey: *Black Edwardians: Black People in Britain, 1901–1914*. Abingdon and New York: Frank Cass. 1998).

Lorimer, Douglas: *Science, Race Relations and Resistance: Britain, 1870–1914 (Studies in Imperialism)* (Manchester: Manchester University Press, 2013).

Longfellow's Hiawatha

Fruhauff, Brad: 'The Lost Work of Longfellow's *Hiawatha*', *The Journal of the Midwest Modern Language Association*, 40/2 (2007), 79–96.

Trachtenberg, Alan: *Shades of Hiawatha: Staging Indians, Making Americans, 1880–1930* (New York: Hill and Wang, 2004).

RECORDINGS OF HIAWATHA

Complete Recording

Hiawatha, Helen Field, Arthur Davies, Bryn Terfel, Welsh National Opera Orchestra and Chorus, Kenneth Alwyn, Argo 2CDs 430 356-2 (1991).

Individual Cantatas

Hiawatha's Wedding Feast, Walter Glynne, Royal Choral Society, Orchestra, Malcolm Sargent, HMV C 1931–4 (1930). Historic recording linked with the Royal Albert Hall productions.

Hiawatha's Wedding Feast, Richard Lewis, Royal Choral Society, Philharmonia Orchestra, Sir Malcolm Sargent, HMV ALP 1899 / ASD 467 (1962).

Hiawatha's Wedding Feast, Anthony Rolfe Johnson, Bournemouth Symphony Chorus and Orchestra, Kenneth Alwyn, EMI EL 27 0145 4 (1984).

The Death of Minnehaha, Elsie Suddaby, Howard Fry, George Baker, Royal Choral Society, Orchestra, Malcolm Sargent, HMV C 2210–13 (1931). Historic recording linked with the Royal Albert Hall productions.

WEB RESOURCES

Samuel Coleridge-Taylor Foundation https://sctf.org.uk. A useful trove of information, albeit not updated for a while.

Samuel Coleridge Taylor and His Music in America, 1900–1912 <https://www.yout ube.com/ watch?v=HebDy-sLdCs>. An informative documentary by the Longfellow Chorus, made for the 2012 anniversary.

INDEX

For the benefit of digital users, indexed terms that span two pages (e.g., 52–53) may, on occasion, appear on only one of those pages.

African American
  purported parallels with Native
    Americans, 33–34, 64–65, 70,
    86–89, 91–92
  reception of Coleridge-Taylor,
    71–81, 108–10
  See also Black musical canon;
    racial uplift; S. Coleridge-Taylor
    Choral Society; spirituals
Alwyn, Kenneth, 111–13
Antcliffe, Herbert, 21–22
anticolonialism, 64–67, 91–93, 106
'art' music, 7–8

Bach, Johann Sebastian, 2–3
'barbarism', as purported musical
    quality, 21
Beckwith, Joseph, 14, 16
Beethoven, Ludwig van, 2–3
Bierstadt, Albert, 62–64
Black Britons 5–7, 92–94
'Black Loyalists', 111
Black musical canon, 109–10. *See also*
  canon (musical)

Bonds, Margaret, 109–10
Brahms, Johannes, 17
Brantlinger, Patrick, 60–61
Brewer, Herbert, 19–20
Brian, Havergal, 90–91
Bridgetower, George, 5
Britten, Benjamin, 4–5
Burleigh, Harry T., 76
Butterworth, Sidney, 94–95

canon (musical), 7–10, 109–10, 111–18.
  See also Black musical canon;
  repertory
Christianity, 57, 58–59, 65–67,
  88–89, 106
Coleridge, Samuel Taylor (poet), 13
Coleridge-Taylor, Avril (Gwendolen)
  (daughter), 93–94
Coleridge-Taylor Choral Society. *See* S.
  Coleridge-Taylor Choral Society
Coleridge-Taylor, Hiawatha (son),
  91, 101
Coleridge-Taylor, Jessie (née
  Walmisley) (wife), 91, 94–95

Coleridge-Taylor, Samuel
  ancestry, 5, 13–14, 93–94, 95–96, 111
  and character of Hiawatha, 89–91
  death, 94–95, 97–100
  early life, 13–16
  posthumous reception in UK, 100–6
  posthumous reception in US, 106–11
  purported African identity, 20–23, 90–96
  purported African quality of his music, 20–23, 94–96, 116–17
  purported American identity, 109–11
  purported English identity, 22–23, 92–95
  purported sympathy for Native Americans, 64–66, 89–91
  student years at RCM, 16–20
  works (other than the *Hiawatha* cantatas):
    A Tale of Old Japan, Op. 76, 89–90, 116–17
    Ballade in A minor, Op. 33, 19–20
    Clarinet Quintet, Op. 10, 17–19
    Fantasiestücke, Op. 5, 12, 17–18, 116–17
    Five Choral Ballads, Op. 54, 24
    Hiawatha, ballet music, Op. 82, 97–100, 113–14
    Hiawathan Sketches, Op. 16, 11–12, 20–21, 24
    Meg Blaine, Op. 48, 116–17
    Nero, incidental music, Op. 62, 113–14
    Nonet, Op. 2, 17–18, 116–17
    Othello, incidental music, Op. 79, 113–14
    Overture to *The Song of Hiawatha*, Op. 30 No. 3, 68–70, 82–86
    Petite Suite de Concert, Op. 77, 68–69, 100–1, 113–14
    Piano Quintet, Op. 1, 17–18
    Symphonic Variations on an African Air, Op. 63, 68–69
    Symphony in A minor, Op. 8, 18–19
    The Atonement, Op. 53, 108–9, 116–17
    The Blind Girl of Castel-Cuille, Op. 43, 24
    Twenty-Four Negro Melodies, Op. 59, 86–87, 116–17
    Violin Concerto, Op. 80, 68–69, 116–17
colonialism, 61–62, 64–67, 91–92, 103–6. *See also* anticolonialism
Cook, Nicholas, 103–5
Cooper, Anna Julia, 80
creolization, 94–96
cultural appropriation, 59–62, 96, 103–5

Delius, Frederick, 23–24
Du Bois, W. E. B., 81–82, 89
Dumas, Alexandre, *père* and *fils*
Dunbar, Paul Laurence, 12, 74, 87–88
Dvořák, Antonín, 16–18, 23–24, 32–34, 76, 86–87

Elgar, Sir Edward, 4–5, 17, 19–20, 23–24, 25–26, 114–15
English Musical Renaissance, 3–5, 110, 111–13
Euba, Akin, 96, 116–17

Fairburn, Thomas Charles, 101
Fisk Jubilee Singers, 74, 83

Fletcher, Percy E., 97–100
Fruhauff, Brad, 55, 60–61

German, Edward, 113–14
Gioia, Dana, 55
Green, Jeffrey, 13
Grieg, Edvard, 17, 69–70
Grove, Sir George, 16–17

Hayes, Roland, 108–9
Hilyer, Andrew F., 81–82
Hilyer, Mamie (Mrs Andrew
    F.), 73–74
Holmans, Benjamin, 13–14
Holst, Gustav, 16–17
Howard University, 106–8
Hughes, Meirion, 66–67
Hurlstone, William, 17

identity, 22–24, 93–94, 95, 110
    See also Coleridge-Taylor, Samuel,
    purported African identity,
    purported American identity,
    purported English identity
Iroquois, 57, 103–5

Jaeger, August Johannes, 11,
    19–20, 22–23, 25–26, 27, 48–
    49, 114–15
Janifer, Ellsworth, 72–73, 110
Joachim, Joseph, 17–19
Johnson, Lola, 74

Kalevala, 58–59

Legge, Robin H., 103–5
Lewis, W. Milton, 88–89
'light' music, 113–15
Longfellow, Henry Wadsworth,
    3–4, 8–9, 11, 23–24, 28, 40–41,
    48–49, 55–64, 66–67, 87–90,
    91–92, 103–5

Lönnrot, Elias, 58–59, 60. See also
    Kalevala
Lotz, Philip Henry, 109–10
Loudin, Frederick, 74

Macpherson, James, 60
marginalization, 5–6, 8–9, 113–18
Martin, Alice Hare (mother), 13
McGinty, Doris, 71, 86–87, 106–8
Mendelssohn, Felix, 2–3, 17–18, 47
metre, 28–30, 57–59
middlebrow, 55, 111–15
modality, 31–33, 36–37, 83

Native American
    culture (depiction and appropria-
    tion of), 53–67, 101–6
    music, 33–34
    See also African American, pur-
    ported parallels with Native
    Americans; Iroquois; Ojibwe;
    Os-Ke-Non-Ton
Novello & Co. (publishers), 1–2,
    17–18, 19–20, 100–1, 103, 114–15
Noyes, Alfred, 89–90

Ojibwe, 56–57, 58–59, 103–5. See also
    Native American, culture
Os-Ke-Non-Ton, 101–3

Pan-African Conference (London,
    1900), 74, 80, 92–93
Parry, Sir Charles Hubert Hastings,
    2–3, 4–5, 111–13
pentatonic, 31–34
Pisani, Michael, 64–65

race, 5–7, 8–9, 91–96, 115–16
Rachmaninov, Sergei, 7–8
racial uplift, 72–81, 109–10
racism, race relations, 6–7, 20–23,
    76–81, 92–93, 118

INDEX   139

repertory, 7–9, 111–13. *See also* canon (musical)
Richards, Paul, 91–92, 94–96
Roosevelt, Theodore, 3–4
Royal Albert Hall, 3–4, 101–3, 111–13
Royal Choral Society (RCS), 101–3
Royal College of Music (RCM), 2–3, 13–16, 111–13

S. Coleridge-Taylor Choral Society (Washington DC), 73–81, 106–8
Sancho, Ignatius, 5
Sargent, Sir Malcolm, 101–3, 111–13
Sayers, W. C. Berwick, 1–2, 13–14, 95
Schiefner, Franz Anton, 58–59
Schoolcraft, Henry Rowe, 56–57
Schumann, Robert and Clara, 17–18
Self, Geoffrey, 91–92
Sierra Leone, 5, 13, 95–96, 111
Sousa, John Philip, 76
spirituals, 33–34, 70, 81–82
‘Nobody knows the trouble I se e, Lord’, 70, 82–86
Stanford, Sir Charles Villiers, 2–3, 16–19, 40–41, 111–13
Stradling, Robert, 66–67
Strauss, Richard, 114–15

Stravinsky, Igor, 2–3
Sullivan, Sir Arthur, 1–2, 4–5, 23–24, 111–13

Taylor, Daniel Peter Hughes (father), 13
Taylor, John (grandfather), 96, 111
Taylor, Samuel Coleridge. *See* Coleridge-Taylor, Samuel
Tchaikovsky, Pyotr Ilyich, 7–8, 17, 21–22
Thomas, Theodore, 71–72
Three Choirs Festival, 19–20, 111–13
Tortolano, William, 94–95
Treble Clef Club (Washington DC), 74
trochaic tetrameter. *See* metre

Vaughan Williams, Ralph, 4–5, 16–17, 111–13
Virgil (Publius Vergilius Maro), 60

Walmisley, Jessie. *See* Coleridge-Taylor, Jessie
Walters, Col. Herbert, 15, 16–17
Washington, Booker T., 5–6, 86–87, 88–89
Whitman, Walt, 56
Wilson, W. Llewellyn, 106–8